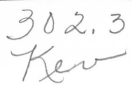

...ished in the United States of America
...owman & Littlefield Education
...ision of Rowman & Littlefield Publishers, Inc.
...lly owned subsidiary of The Rowman & Littlefield Publishing Group, Inc.
...orbes Boulevard, Suite 200, Lanham, Maryland 20706
...owmaneducation.com

...Road
...h PL6 7PY
...Kingdom

...ry Cataloguing in Publication Information Available

...ongress Cataloging-in-Publication Data

...eline M., 1968–
...ut bullying: what everyone should know / Meline Kevorkian and
...na.

...-1-57886-849-0 (cloth: alk. paper)
...886-849-1 (cloth: alk. paper)
...-1-57886-896-4
...886-896-3
...D'Antona, Robin, 1946– II. Title. III. Title: One hundred one
...g.
...2008

2008014129

1 0 1 F A C[T]
A B O U[T]
B U L L Y I[NG]

What Everyone Sh[ould]

Meline Kevo[rkian]
Robin D'[Antona]

ROWMAN

Lanham

Publ[ished]
by R[owman]
A Div[ision]
A who[lly]
4501 [...]
www.r[owman...]

Estover [...]
Plymout[h]
United [Kingdom]

Copyrigh[t]

All rights [reserved]
in a retriev[al]
mechanica[l]
of the publ[isher]

British Libr[ary]

Library of [Congress]

Kevorkian, M[eline]
101 facts abo[ut bullying]
Robin D'Anto[na]
p. cm.
ISBN-13: 978[...]
ISBN-10: 1-57[...]
eISBN-13: 978[...]
eISBN-10: 1-5[...]
1. Bullying. I. [...]
facts about bullyi[ng]
BF637.B85K48
302.3—dc22

CONTENTS

INTRODUCTION

Today educators, parents, grandparents, social workers, law enforcement officers, psychologists, and all those involved in the lives of children and young adults are faced with issues of bullying. Along with the life pressures that our students face today, bullying ranks high on the list of tremendous challenges facing kids. This challenge has a great impact on their academic achievement, social interactions, and overall well-being.

Given the stakes, bullying prevention is a key responsibility for all adults. Educating and protecting kids from the abuse associated with bullying must be a priority. Learning environments should be designed with a focus on bullying prevention. The key to bullying prevention is creating a caring and positive school culture.

The first and most crucial step to bullying prevention and promoting peace is to separate the myths and facts and to gain awareness of what research says about bullying and its prevention. While there is an abundance of information on bullying, not all of it is based in quality research. In order to set the example for kids and to make any bullying-prevention plan successful, there must be a fundamental belief that bullying is a serious problem.

In addition, the stakeholders must feel empowered to act when bullying behavior is encountered. This book is designed to break down what the research says about bullying, including cyberbullying, and its effects. It is our hope that this book will give you the practical information to reduce or even eliminate bullying.

❶

MYTHS AND FACTS

Fact #1 Bullying is a reality! (Dake, Price, & Telljohann, 2003)

Gaining the Peaceful Edge . . . Acknowledging the fact that bullying is a serious issue confronting our children.

Research has suggested that many students are and will continue to be bullied. We live in a social world, and this is especially true in schools. One hundred percent of children are touched by bullying as a victim, perpetrator, or bystander. Bullying is a reality that must be recognized and addressed. Bullying and teasing are not simply a part of growing up.

These behaviors should not be tolerated or dismissed, especially when their consequences reach far beyond the classroom. The research is consistent that bullying and teasing create a fear and concern for safety that retards and stops the learning process and may have long-lasting negative effects.

In a recent study, 77 percent of students said they have been bullied, and 14 percent of those who have been bullied said they have experienced severe reactions to the abuse. According to *Hostile Hallways: Bullying, Teasing, and Sexual Harassment in School* (2001), in a national sample, 83 percent of boys and 79 percent of girls said they have been bullied.

Approximately 76 percent of this was nonphysical and approximately 60 percent was under the teacher's nose. More than half the students want to know how to stop it. Fifty percent of kids have received comments about their sexuality. Third graders through high schoolers say "faggot," "you're so gay," and "homo," with little or no regard for the pain they may cause. Such verbal abuse has become far too tolerable and often dismissed as kids' jargon.

Fact #2 Many children are bullied in school.

Gaining the Peaceful Edge . . . Think about the fact that 55 percent of eight- to eleven-year-olds tell us that bullying is a problem, and then consider the children in your life.

According to a study conducted by Nickelodeon (2001), 74 percent of seven- to eleven-year-olds and 86 percent of twelve- to fifteen-year-olds indicated that children were bullied or teased in their schools. Additionally, 55 percent of eight- to eleven-year-olds and 68 percent of twelve- to fifteen-year-olds said that bullying was a "big problem" for people their age.

We seem to have full agreement that talking about drugs, alcohol, and peer pressure is a must for our youth. Our children are very vulnerable and can be overwhelmed and intimidated by general peer and school pressures. When bullying and teasing enter the equation, schools become a place of survival rather than a place of learning. Too often, our children are feeling like nobody can help when it comes to bullying. They often see it happening and don't know what to do to resolve the problem.

We have all seen infomercials and ads that talk about the importance of talking with our children about drugs and alcohol. We must do the same thing when it comes to protecting their self esteem, overall well-being, and sense of belonging. Bullying involves both physical and mental components and has the potential to cause long-term damage equal to or greater than the effects of drugs and alcohol. In many cases, drugs and alcohol may be utilized to escape from the hurt and torment associated with bullying and teasing.

One of the best things that we can do to combat bullying is to ask kids what they think. When we ask them about their school day we must ask about the unstructured part of the day. Ask questions such as, Who did you sit with at lunch? How often are kids bullied in your school? What happens to kids who are bullied? What happens to bullies?

There are so many pressures on educators to help children succeed in school and reach their potential. Yet, the key to success in school is eliminating bullying and building a culture of respect where all stakeholders are valued and diversity is embraced.

Fact #3 It happens in front of adults! (Hazler, Carney, & Granger, 2006)

Gaining the Peaceful Edge . . . Be aware that most bullying incidents happen in less than a minute and often in front of adults.

Hazler, Miller, Carney, and Green (2001) analyzed adult recognition of what constitutes bullying in schools. The results showed that physical conflicts were more often rated as bullying, even if they did not fit the definition of bullying, and that the repetitive nature of bullying is easily overlooked if it is perceived as a fair fight.

Educators and all those involved in education must receive the proper training to be able to identify what differentiates bullying from normal fighting or childhood banter. Bullying is a purposeful action that is intended to injure and involves both physical and mental components and imbalance of power.

Administrators and teachers tell us that classroom discipline and sustaining a school culture where all children can learn and grow emotionally and intellectually is a difficult task. The challenge is to foster a culture of respect by being an example of how to treat others; this is often lacking in teacher-education programs. We become masters of the curricular and pedagogy but may not get the details necessary to promoting the highest character and motivation for academic success.

Parents are the first and principal teachers of children. Research supports the need for a successful relationship between schools and parents. Bullying prevention requires that all stakeholders be involved. It is very difficult for educators to confront parents when a child's academics or discipline plummets. Just imagine how difficult it must be to discuss the possibilities of a child being a victim or bully.

Additionally, it is going to take everyone working together to help bystanders, both children and adults, to have the courage to and know how to intervene. Parents must also really listen to their children and take the time to entertain what they are saying, investigate the circumstances, and support their children when they reach out for assistance. "Just ignore it" does not assist a child who is suffering silently at the hands of others.

A child's reaching out is not always verbal. We must be aware of the signs that a child may be suffering. Evidence of bullying may not come home on a test paper or a progress report. You must check your children from head to toe and inside out for signs of abuse, which may come in mental and physical forms. We hear too often that kids didn't reach out to adults because they were ashamed, afraid, or knew there was nothing the adults could do.

Fact #4 Both boys and girls are involved in bullying. (Brinson, 2005)

Gaining the Peaceful Edge . . . Understand that both genders engage in social bullying behavior.

Both boys and girls involve themselves in the unfair treatment of others. Girls often tend to be hurtful and band together to isolate certain students.

The days of thinking little girls are all "sugar and spice and everything nice" are long gone. Girls share the ability to bully and tease their classmates with their male counterparts. Additionally, we must steer away from the belief that boys will be boys and demand that all classmates treat each other with respect and dignity. The rates of girls involving themselves in fighting and violence are on the rise. Hence, the "picture" of a bully is fuzzy. Exclusion, gossiping, and teasing seem to be some of the favorite pastimes of our girls.

While we hear of these incidents mostly from girls, we need to understand that it can happen among boys as well. Choosing to exclude another child from a group can be devastating to the victim regardless of gender. Boys tend to do it in according to group (i.e., athletes and nonathletes), while girls tend to bully according to their social status (i.e., popular vs. nonpopular).

Spreading rumors is another way that children bully their peers. With the easy access to electronic communication, this form of bullying has become quite prevalent. The anonymity of electronic means such as the computer and text messaging make it very easy to bully another unsuspecting student.

Having a strong defense is a requirement for getting through the school day. The last thing you want to be is a tattletale, so you hone in on your "nasty" skills to be able to avoid being the victim. It has been said that "nice girls" will not and don't survive very long. Part of the middle school and high school transition is learning how to come back when someone attacks you verbally.

The fear of becoming the next victim engenders girls to isolate the girl being targeted. This leaves the victim feeling targeted, isolated, and alone to suffer the hurt and humiliation. These behaviors of exclusion and humiliation toward another student can leave long-term emotional scars. Feelings of isolation and a lack of confidence are often rooted in social bullying.

Fact #5 Bullying is a worldwide problem! (Kuntsche et al., 2006)

Gaining the Peaceful Edge . . . Discuss what could happen elsewhere to gain insight into your child's world.

Unfortunately, research illustrates that bullying is prevalent not only in the United States but throughout the world.

Children everywhere involve themselves in and are exposed to bullying. Whenever and wherever children and teens gather together, you will unfortunately find bullying. As active organizers of an international conference on the best practices of bullying prevention, it is astonishing to hear from colleagues around the globe seeking the "magic formula" to bullying prevention.

The stress associated with this epidemic shatters all borders as well as socioeconomic classes. Educators, parents, and students may feel like they do not have anything in common with people in other parts of the world, but when it comes to bullying they do. Additionally, where we are from, our customs and traditions, religious beliefs, and the color of our skin may be used as a reason to bully.

International researchers have demonstrated that bullying in schools is universal. In every nation, peer pressure exists, but it doesn't always have to be negative. If we could turn peer pressure around, it could teach tolerance and place the pressure to accept and even elevate diversity. Parents and educators play an important role in this, because the influence of adults goes a long way.

We know that parents who are alcoholics have a greater risk of raising children who are alcoholics. Similarly, parents who use drugs have a greater risk of raising children who use drugs. In the same vein, children who are exposed to jokes and innuendoes regarding race, religion, gender, and sexual identity, to name a few, will most likely carry these beliefs into their daily lives, in and out of the classroom.

Talking with children about bullying in other parts of the world can be helpful. Often through these conversations you can better understand the child's own personal experiences with bullying.

Across the globe we must have consistent bullying prevention standards for the treatment and respect of others.

Fact #6 Bullying is serious, even at a young age!

Gaining the Peaceful Edge . . . From the youngest ages, children need to be taught to be kind to each other. This is the best protection against bullying.

In 2006, Finkelhor, Turner, and Ormrod examined the presumption that victimizations involving younger children are simply the result of child's play that has gotten out of hand. Surveying and interviewing children and youth aged two to seventeen and their caregivers revealed that peer victimizations between young children are no less serious than older youth peer victimizations. Trauma symptom levels were high with all types of victimization.

Preschool teachers and administrators tell us they are shocked at the number of incidences linked to bullying in the preschool years, such as children as young as two asking if they are ugly or fat. These behaviors not only can have serious long-term effects but they also escalate as the child grows older.

We must be certain that we model kindness and respect for rules. The stress and anguish related to bullying is not just for middle and high school students. Preschool students have come home upset about being left out or ridiculed by their peers.

One of the main goals of preschool is to instill a love of learning and an excitement for school. Through play, children can explore and learn about their environment. The classroom is their micro society where children learn to navigate socially. It is important that the classroom be a safe place for children to try out various roles. Patterns set here are often the roots of lessons that, once learned, inform behavior in later life.

It is distressing when young children are preoccupied with worries about "getting picked on." Research supports that children establish their attitudes toward school in the first nine years of life. Bullying may impact their view of how they belong in school and the effort they will employ in the future in their educational career.

It is most important that children's first years are nurturing and provide a sense of belonging in their school. The educational setting should foster their self-esteem, cater to their sense of curiosity, and motivate them to learn.

Fact #7 Bullying is violence and a human-rights issue. (Kirman, 2004)

Gaining the Peaceful Edge . . . Recognize that bullying is not child's play and should never be dismissed as such.

Some sociologists recognize that bullying is a human-rights issue. The notion that all students must feel safe in school is one that can be addressed by focusing on constructive values, knowledge, and attitudes.

Research suggests that many children skip school for fear of being bullied or teased at school. These staggering statistics indicate the immensity of the problem of bullying. Every child has the right to attend school, have a sense of belonging, and feel safe. When children miss school for fear of being bullied, they miss opportunities to learn. Additionally, when students are unable to focus on their academics out of fear for their safety and the risk of being bullied, they are also robbed of their opportunity to learn. We know that as adults, when we are preoccupied with fear and anxiety, we are unable to focus on the other aspects of our lives. Children are no different.

Bullying and teasing are roadblocks to learning that deny the right to a safe place to learn. School culture must be developed to foster respect and provide barriers to destructive behaviors like bullying by providing core values that clarify what is acceptable treatment of peers, teachers, and all members of the school community. A child's character must be nurtured and developed just as their intellect. We must foster empathy in our children. The exposure to acts of kindness, charity to those in need, and tolerance and patience for the differences in everyone must equalize the negative exposure to violence and lack of respect depicted too often in the media.

Community service is a step in the right direction, but we must help our kids experience the joy, happiness, and fulfillment associated with giving, sharing, and helping. Attention should be focused on those that do the right thing and set the example, rather than on those who do not. Unfortunately, the negative things are given too much attention, even when negative consequences are involved.

Fact #8 Even friends can be bullies. (Kevorkian, 2006)

Gaining the Peaceful Edge . . . Talk about the definition of a good friend as well as the difference between acquaintances, buddies, and true friends.

Bullying behavior is not confined to the "class" bully. It can occur within a child's circle of friends. Hence, children need guidance in fostering positive relationships and selecting friends.

The group of kids that a child surrounds themselves with determines a lot of their happiness and a lot of their tears. We must discuss the qualities of a friend and the possibility that not everyone fits into that category. As children grow and develop, their friends play a crucial role in their lives. What happens between classmates and peers determines how they feel about school and themselves. How their peers see them is often how they see themselves.

Children and teens can be very cruel at times. Helping children surround themselves with happy, supportive friends will help them feel happy and supported. The expression "you are known by the company you keep" seems to be pretty accurate.

This is the same when it comes to kids who bully others. If a particular child is constantly upsetting and ridiculing another child, it would be most wise for an adult to intervene and suggest a new friend or circle of friends.

Conversations about being and determining friends should be held on a regular basis. Parents should know who their children's friends are, and teachers should pay attention to the dynamics in the classroom and unstructured time. Educators should diffuse themes of friendship into the classroom whenever possible. Children should be taught to differentiate between constructive criticism, friendly advice, and outright bullying.

Our children need to understand that a friend that makes them cry is not a friend. They should also understand the difference between peer pressure and outright bullying, although sometimes it may be just a fine line. Cite examples from your childhood and experiences that will shed light on your child's circumstances. Remember our children are only children, and at times we must define and explain things so they can understand the true nature of friendship. This is how they learn.

Fact #9 The average episode of bullying lasts only thirty-seven seconds. Teachers notice or intervene in only one in twenty-five incidents.

Gaining the Peaceful Edge . . . Teach bystanders to recognize and respond to bullying incidents.

Bullying does not have to be prolonged or elaborate. Observations of children on a playground noted that not only did bullying take less than a minute but also in most cases teachers hardly noticed and, for a variety of reasons, rarely intervened.

A few moments may have a profound impact on a child or young adult's self-esteem. Teachers must be given the tools and feel empowered and prepared to step in and assist. Many educators are unaware of bullying plans and policies and are uncertain of their role in intervention strategies. Since bullying incidents happen so frequently it is understandable that adults are often not aware of what is happening. Children and teens have reported that bullying is a big problem that happens "right under the teacher's nose." They have shared that they don't tell adults because they don't think the adults can actually help or may even make it worse.

Bystanders, both adults and peers, are afraid to step in and assist the target being bullied. We have witnessed classrooms where students have been humiliated and students and the teacher pretended not to hear. Educators need training on bullying prevention to increase their ability and confidence to intervene and set the tone that bullying will not be tolerated without retribution. Additionally, educators must be trained to recognize the signs that a student has been bullied and to provide critical supervision in these unstructured times.

We as parents are guilty of the same. Haven't you ever witnessed your teenage child hang up the receiver after a one-minute phone conversation and storm off into their bedroom? Then we approach them and ask what is wrong and they say "nothing." We must watch for reactions and changes in mood and inquire further. It is time for teachers, parents, and others involved in the lives of children to take a stand and make a difference. Intervening and reacting are two different things, and we must learn to react and intervene because staying silent is like giving a seal of approval.

Fact #10 Bullying does not build character; it is not just a part of growing up.

Gaining the Peaceful Edge . . . Kindness, not hurt and humiliation, builds character .

This is an age-old attitude that has fostered bullying behavior. It is important to move beyond that conception and consider the research that shows that children who are continually victimized by bullying become socially withdrawn.

Character education is about increasing respect for self and others. There is no place for bullying in character building. Children need role models that foster honesty, trust, kindness, appreciation, tolerance, and respect.

The days of dismissing bullying as "boys will be boys" or "girls are just mean" are over. When we dismiss bullying as child's play we are leaving children and schools unprotected. The effects from bullying may be long-term and devastating. Children have the right to be in school and feel safe and that they belong. Adults may be held accountable for deliberate indifference to and failure to protect someone who has reported suspicions of bullying. Reasonable precautions must be made to protect and prevent bullying. Remember, bullying is purposeful and intended to injure, is carried out repeatedly, and has the potential to cause long-term damage.

You have probably heard the quote "what doesn't kill you makes you stronger," which is absolutely untrue. What bullying does is tear down your self-esteem, make you question your self-worth, and, in some cases, make you want to give up on life. Bullies leave you feeling a loss of control in every aspect in your life, which in turn affects sleep patterns, eating habits, school work, social activity, and life in general. Perpetrators must be stopped and taught empathy. Our children need to be rewarded for kindness; being good and doing the right thing should get as much attention as disciplining negative behaviors is given.

REFERENCES

American Association of University Women. (2001). *Hostile hallways: Bullying, teasing, and sexual harassment in schools.* Washington, DC: Author.

Brinson, S. (2005). Boys don't tell on sugar-and-spice-but-not-so-nice girl bullies. *Reclaiming Children and Youth, 14*(3), 169.

Finkelhor, D., Turner, H., & Ormrod, R. (2006). Kid's stuff: The nature and impact of peer and sibling violence on younger and older children. *Child Abuse & Neglect, 30*(12), 1,401.

Hazler, Carney, J., & Granger, D. (2006). Integrating biological measures into the study of bullying. *Journal of Counseling and Development, 84*(3), 298.

Hazler, R., & Miller, D. (2001). Adult recognition of school bullying situations. *Educational Research, 43*(2), 133–46.

Kevorkian, M. (2006). *Preventing bullying: Helping kids form positive relationships.* Lanham, MD: Rowman & Littlefield Education.

Kirman, J. (2004). Using the theme of bullying to teach about human rights in the social studies curriculum. *McGill Journal of Education, 39*(3), 327.

Kuntsche, E., Pickett, W., Overpeck, M., Craig, W., Boyce, W., & de Matos, M. G. (2006). Television viewing and forms of bullying among adolescents from eight countries. *Journal of Adolescent Health, 39*(6), 908.

Nickelodeon. (2001). Bullying, discrimination and sexual pressures: "Big problems" for today's tweens and younger kids; parents often wait for their kids to raise tough issues [electronic version]. Retrieved January 22, 2008, from www.talkingwithkids.org/nickelodeon/pr-3-8-01.htm.

2

BULLYING DEFINED

Fact #11 Bullying is different than "normal" childhood teasing! (Hazler, Carney, & Granger, 2006)

Gaining the Peaceful Edge . . . Teasing and taunting are bullying when the behavior is not reciprocal.

Sometimes bullying is viewed as harmless and a normal part of growing up. However, it is not a part of normal child conflict and should never be dismissed as such. Essentially, bullying occurs whenever it lowers another's self-esteem and is one-sided. Research supports the idea that bullying interferes with the learning process and may have long-term negative effects.

Bullying should never be tolerated, and we must do everything possible to prevent and minimize bullying at school. There has been increasing attention on bullying because of acts of school violence around the country. We shouldn't wait for some tragedy in the news but rather should bring awareness to the prevalence and seriousness of bullying in our schools. The consequences associated with bullying are far too grave to ignore.

Many adults are unable to recognize what is bullying versus normal conflicts among students. We can no longer believe that sticks and stones will break our bones but names will never hurt us. The consequences in the school may be school violence as well as suicide. Remember that bullying is done with intent to harm and is done in repeatedly with an imbalance of power. Children dealing the bullying are at risk for long-lasting and negative effects.

If a seventh grader walked into a classroom and pulled a beer out of their backpack, I'm certain that any adult who witnessed this would take immediate action to confiscate the alcohol from the student and make sure that the student was sent to the office to face severe consequences. Unfortunately, when students bully and humiliate their peers, most often there is no action taken by the adults and no consequences from the school administration. There are some schools where educators and parents believe that bullying has been around for a long time and it is just kids being kids.

Fact #12 Names can hurt you! (Giard, 2006)

Gaining the Peaceful Edge . . . When a child is constantly called derogatory names, the child may believe that the names are accurate.

Name-calling that makes a child feel anxious, angry, or unworthy may diminish a student's drive for education. Many times this will happen in front of their peers. Teasing can have severe and even lifelong consequences. Exposed to this type of abuse for a long time, these children may become incapable of reaching their potential. They actually feel like they deserve to be picked on. Kids are left feeling like they are not important and don't belong in the school. Physical fights are short lived and a few bruises will eventually heal, but name-calling and mean acts have a lasting impression. These names may spread rapidly in the virtual world. With the click of a button, these words may be spread to an entire class or through the school in moments.

These victimized kids don't know where to turn. When bystanders—kids or adults—stand by and take no action, it reinforces to kids that no one can help. These children are left feeling unworthy and too often blame themselves for the actions of the bullies. Adults need to learn how to respond and how to assist children who may be victimized by name-calling. We could all benefit from the old saying, "if you don't have anything nice to say, don't say anything at all." In fact, this would be a great school rule. Constant reminders about respect and the treatment of others should be part of the daily routine.

Adults serve as role models, and we must make sure that we are sending the right messages in everything that we say and do. Teachers, counselors, administrators, and parents who interact with children every day must be certain to model kindness. They need to become familiar with identifying when children are playing, joking, and fighting or when bullying is occurring. We must pay attention to the difference.

Somehow when children enter about fourth grade, the word "gay" becomes a favorite. There seems to be little concern given to the fact that calling a peer that name is hurtful and wrong. By fifth grade, the improper and rude vocabulary grows. We must teach children that what they see is just as important as what they do. Children believe what they hear repeatedly, and if they hear over and over again that they're stupid or that they don't belong, they will believe it.

Fact #13 Adults must watch for the signs that a child is being bullied! (Kevorkian, 2006)

Gaining the Peaceful Edge . . . Children who are being bullied may seem withdrawn, depressed, and nervous and may show changes in behavior.

Educators should watch for signs that indicate a child may be bullied and provide the support and guidance needed to break the destructive pattern (Schnohr & Niclasen, 2006; Hazler, Miller, Carney, & Green, 2001). Parents are the first and most essential teachers.

We must really know our children and watch for any signs of stress. Sometimes they are so occupied worrying about what's going to happen in the school day that their concentration suffers and grades go down. Other bullied children appear ill and request to stay home.

As adults, stress makes us feel uncomfortable, nervous, unsafe, and mistrusting. We cannot think clearly and often feel anxious. We become restless, lose sleep, and behave quite irritably. We may experience phantom aches and pains, have stomachaches and headaches. Children experience many of the same feelings. The difference is that they do not have the same frame of reference as adults. They do not understand that these feelings are part of life and need not necessarily be permanent.

Children are resilient; however, they need to understand that a situation that is causing difficulty will pass. Essentially, children often don't understand the connections between their unsettling emotions and physical symptoms. They do not realize that their feelings can be the cause of their physical symptoms, moodiness, and ill temper.

Make sure that a child feels good about coming to school and that they feel confident that they belong and are worthy to be in the school. Educators should be trained in the signs that a child is under stress, as well as how to differentiate between bullying and other forms of youthful play. It is good to know your children's friends. When needed, ask your child's teacher who he/she spends her time with. We must help children academically, as well as socially, and help them find their place in the school.

Fact #14 It is important to know the difference between bullying and other types of conflict between children. (Bullock, 2002)

Gaining the Peaceful Edge . . . Not all conflict is bullying—and adults as well as children need to know the difference!

Children have a lot of interaction and, in fact, in the first years of schooling spend a lot of time learning about sharing and getting along. In fact, we spend a lot of time reinforcing those lessons in kindergarten, but those lessons disappear from the curriculum as children move to the upper grades. It is imperative that we fit reminders at every grade to help children understand conflict and how to handle it.

Children and adults need to understand what bullying is, how to identify it, and what can be done to prevent it. If adults and children understand what bullying is, they have a better chance they will recognize it when they see it or experience it for themselves. Right now there are children being bullied that don't even know it, and adults are watching and, by their lack of action, are giving their stamp of approval without even knowing it. True efforts for bullying prevention require action on the part of bystanders, both adults and children. If they can't identify bullying from normal kid conflict, it will retard any prevention efforts. The overall culture of the school will be compromised; academic achievement will suffer and perhaps even weaken school safety efforts.

For any bullying-prevention effort to be successful, there must be a belief among all stakeholders, school administrator, teachers, counselors, parents, and students that bullying is serious and wrong under any circumstances and will be addressed. When everyone is trained in what to look for, we'll have a better chance of identifying bullying versus regular kid confrontation and putting a stop to it.

Fact #15 Sibling violence is as serious as peer-on-peer violence. In other words, when the violence is between siblings, regardless of age, it can be as traumatic as if it involved a peer. (Finkelhor, Turner, & Ormrod, 2006)

Gaining the Peaceful Edge . . . Research clearly indicates the importance of parent education in reducing bullying among children. Parents need to be diligent regarding the nature of the interpersonal relationships of siblings.

Parents need to really take a good look at their children and the behaviors they display. One of the main jobs of being a parent is to know what's happening in their children's school and social lives. Additionally, we must serve as the constant reminder of our expectations for their character and nurture their value system, moral development, and general manners. When our children hear us being sarcastic and rude to other people, they are certain to follow.

We must exemplify what we want in our children, because they are always watching the adults they come in contact with. They learn how to disagree and otherwise how to treat others by the way that we treat people. When we treat others with kindness and compassion, they are likely to do the same. When we treat others poorly and belittle others, they are likely to do the same; when we allow them to treat siblings and family members with disrespect, and do not intervene when siblings belittle others, they see it as okay. Remember that children are always watching adults. Adults should model how they want their kids to treat others, especially in the home.

When they see how you talk to other members of the family, they learn how to communicate. If they see you yelling and screaming in a demeaning manner, they will also do the same. It is very difficult to be a parent or an educator, because we must always walk the walk and talk the talk. Remember, kids are always watching and absorbing how we interact and behave in various situations. Children follow in the footsteps of their parents. We have heard the expression, "the fruit doesn't fall far from the tree." Make sure the fruit you produce is sweet, kind, and nurturing.

Fact #16 Bullying can be direct—hitting, pushing, kicking, and general hurtful threatening behaviors and gestures—but it always involves an imbalance of power. (Craig, Pepler, & Atlas, 2000)

Gaining the Peaceful Edge . . . Always consider balance of power when determining if you are dealing with bullying, roughhousing, or just fighting.

Kids can be very creative in the ways they choose to hurt one another. They can give wedgies, push with their backpacks, use bathroom time to push, shove, peek, poke, and verbally humiliate. Just ask kids to talk about ways in which kids clash, and they will stun you with the extent and creativity of their arsenal.

The definition of bullying says that negative behaviors need to be repeated and and with the intent to do harm. But any negative and hurtful behaviors become bullying when there is an imbalance of power. This happens when a student is being victimized and cannot defend himself or herself.

Not all bad behavior is bullying. Kids can still mix it up and get involved in a fight. If they are truly equal peers, this is not bullying behavior. In these instances, they begin as friends and have a disagreement that escalates into a fight. This can be anything from physical fighting to threatening to fight. But the difference here is that these disputes can be resolved. Once that happens, the children continue to be friends.

In the same manner, kids can roughhouse. This behavior, also known as horseplay, is genial physical jostling that occurs when both students willingly participate. The children are of equal power. They begin as friends and end as friends. This is not bullying. Rather, it is friendly playful behavior. Roughhousing is something that happens on playgrounds everywhere and is a normal part of childhood. However since this behavior can easily escalate into fighting, it is advisable to closely supervise children. Some teachers talk with children about roughhousing and ask them to set some basic ground rules. That will give them the opportunity to think about the difference between roughhousing and fighting and to set some acceptable parameters to avoid escalation into fighting.

The imbalance occurs when one student is more powerful than the other. For instance, when one student is older, larger, smarter, and more popular than the other, there is an imbalance of power. Basically, it is about a playing field that is not level, enabling one student to unfairly take advantage of the other.

Fact #17 Bullying can be indirect—gossip, rumors, and damaging another student's reputation. Indirect bullying includes getting someone else to bully a victim. (Leckie, 1998; Wheeler, 2004)

Gaining the Peaceful Edge . . . While this form of bullying is very difficult to pinpoint, indirect bullying needs to be taken very seriously.

Indirect bullying can include:

- Getting another person to assault someone
- Spreading rumors
- Getting someone to deliberately exclude someone from a group or activity
- Cyberbullying by second parties
- Mean gestures such as rolling of eyes or averting eyes to ignore someone
- Getting someone to steal or hide a person's belongings

It is very common for kids, particularly in groups, to isolate a peer and to bully them indirectly. It is also an example of the "seven-second bullying"—that is, the average time it takes for a student to be victimized. It can happen in an instant, and the teacher or adult present never sees a thing. Just imagine how quickly a roll of the eyes or a sharp look away can happen. The end result is devastation for the target from being repeatedly snubbed and insulted.

Another common form of indirect bullying is stealing or hiding another student's belongings. When this occurs, the bully's defense is that it was just a joke to hide the object and to watch the outcome. But jokes at the expense of another, particularly when the target is repeatedly singled out, are bullying.

One of the most insidious forms of bullying is spreading rumors. Today this is most often done on a cell phone or the Internet. They can buddy chat with a group or instant message (IM) to a cell phone and the means of communication grows almost daily. Along with the ability to have secret communication comes increased opportunity to gossip and spread rumors.

Under the cloak of privacy, anything can be said, and there is no way to see the result of those actions. These communications are completely anonymous, and with that anonymity comes a lack of empathy. Reduced or even a complete lack of empathy is the cornerstone of bullying behavior.

Fact #18 Physical bullying is the most common and most likely to demand a response from adults. (Stewart, 2007)

Gaining the Peaceful Edge . . . When bullying becomes physical, it comes to the attention of adults. The key to reducing this form of bullying is to intervene long before that happens.

Bullying most often is an escalating experience. It can begin with a look or gesture or perhaps an indirect act such as deliberately avoiding contact with another student. These activities, when unchecked, will most often escalate into physical bullying. In addition, and more importantly, allowing these behaviors erodes a school's safe climate.

School becomes a fearful place for not only the target of this behavior but also the bystanders. They know that with any small turn of events they can become the target. This impacts their behavior so that they often will follow the lead of the student who chooses to bully.

At the same time, as long as the nonphysical bullying goes on unchecked, it will, as we have noted, escalate. This will lead to actually hurting another. The process of acceleration often is gradual while at the same time, it erodes the bully's feelings of empathy. This makes the bullying more satisfying and rewarding.

There is no impetus for the bullying to stop. This becomes the basis for the continuation for the behavior. It is often much more complex than the single incident of physical bullying that is brought to the attention of a teacher or other adult.

Jeremy was a seventh grade boy who was not adept in gym class. He was usually the last one chosen for teams. Kids in his class would mimic how he handled the basketball, and his team members they would play "keep away" so he would not get a turn with the ball. The teacher told the kids to play fair—they all were equal parts of a team. But Jeremy began to hate to go to gym. At first he would ask to go to the nurse, then he would develop physical symptoms to avoid school altogether.

Then the bullying became physical. One boy deliberately hit him in the face with the ball. Jeremy was so angry, he hit the boy back. At that point the teacher intervened, but the emotions were running deep, and this was much more than the single exchange that brought the teacher into the mix. If there had been intervention at an earlier point, all of this could have been avoided.

Fact #19 Verbal bullying goes to the core of how we treat each other. (Freedman, 2002)

Gaining the Peaceful Edge . . . Verbal bullying begins when children and people in general do not treat each other with respect. The key to handling this is for adults to model positive behavior. Examples are a very powerful way to send a message.

Verbal bullying includes name-calling, insulting, making racist comments, and constant teasing. Verbal bullies use words to hurt or humiliate another person. This type of bullying is the easiest to inflict on other children. It is quick and to the point and can occur in the least amount of time available. Its effects can be more devastating in some ways than physical bullying, because there are no visible scars.

We need to talk to children about how they respond and react to their peers by stressing the value of respect. Talking and acting in respectful ways helps to give children the opportunity to recognize and value respect. This can be pointed out to them in many different ways, but the most powerful way to teach children is by our own example.

This brings us to a very delicate point that adults may find hard to hear. We have to examine ourselves before we can judge children about their behavior. When adults bully each other they are setting a negative example for children. Under those circumstances, all the words of wisdom regarding the virtue of respect are overshadowed by destructive modeling.

Adults can also bully kids when they are dealing with bullying behavior. While this sounds absurd, it happens when adults use threats and intimidation to deal with these situations. We have to think of what we want from a child and then behave in that manner. It is common sense, yet, in the heat of the moment adults often misuse their power and essentially bully the child who is a bully. Therefore we always must be mindful of how we respond to others, as it will impact children and their future relationships.

Fact #20 Children who use their friendships to bully others are called relational bullies. (Bullock, 2002)

Gaining the Peaceful Edge . . . We all need to recognize that the use of relationships to manipulate, harm, embarrass, or humiliate another is relational bullying.

Relational bullies can cause hurt and damage beyond description. They use their relationships to hurt their peers. They can do this by excluding a target in order to cut them off from their social connections. This rejection can leave the victim feeling lonely and isolated. Students ages twelve to fourteen or in middle school tend to be particularly vulnerable to this type of bullying because of their need for affiliation and social connection at that stage of their emotional development.

Often this type of bullying can be linked to verbal bullying. Rumors, criticisms, nasty comments, judgments, and disapproval typify this behavior. To make matters worse, this verbal bullying can spill over into the world of media. This is extremely serious because kids can connect with many, many more of their peers, instantaneously causing more damage than ever. However, insults and exclusion are nonetheless painful and equally as devastating regardless of the mode of contact.

The key to dealing with these behaviors is for everyone—both students and adults—to recognize the behavior. This can be as simple as asking the question "Do these actions or these words hurt anyone?" Basically it is about how we treat one another and determining if the action is kind and supportive or mean and destructive. It is about building friendship skills—that is, teaching children to recognize friends and to behave in the manner they expect from their friends.

Bystanders have a pivotal role in relational bullying. Their participation in this behavior is exactly what promulgates and spreads this form of bullying. By teaching kids to choose not to participate, the circulation of the rumors or negative feedback is greatly reduced. As adults we need to take all reports of exclusion or relational bullying seriously and respond immediately to minimize the damage. By using this two-pronged approach, much suffering, humiliation, and hurt can be eliminated.

REFERENCES

Bullock, J. (2002). Bullying among children. *Childhood Education, 78*(3), 130.

Craig, W. M., Pepler, D., & Atlas, R. (2000). Observations of bullying in the playground and in the classroom. *School Psychology International, 21*(1), 22.

Finkelhor, D., Turner, H., & Ormrod, R. (2006). Kid's stuff: The nature and impact of peer and sibling violence on younger and older children. *Child Abuse & Neglect, 30*(12), 1,401.

Freedman, J. (2002). *Easing the teasing: Helping your child cope with name-calling, ridicule, and verbal bullying.* Blacklick, OH: McGraw-Hill Order Services.

Giard, M. (2006). Bullycide prevention sqilxwcut, through filmmaking: An urban native youth performance project. *Canadian Journal of Native Education, 29*(1), 58.

Hazler, Carney, J., & Granger, D. (2006). Integrating biological measures into the study of bullying. *Journal of Counseling and Development, 84*(3), 298.

Hazler, R., & Miller, D. (2001). Adult recognition of school bullying situations. *Educational Research, 43*(2), 133–46.

Kevorkian, M. (2006). *Preventing bullying: Helping kids form positive relationships.* Lanham, MD: Rowman & Littlefield Education.

Leckie, B. (1998). Girls, bullying behaviors and peer relationships: The double edged sword of exclusion and rejection. Paper presented at the Annual Conference of the Australian Association for Research in Education. From 0-www-uk1.csa.com.novacat.nova.edu/ids70/view_record.php?id=0&recnum=9&log=next&SID=3957cf5a85915ac701d29ae06e925cbb&mark_id=view%3A12%2C8%2C9&mark=8.

Schnohr, C., & Niclasen, B. (2006). Bullying amoung Greenlandic schoolchildren: development since 1994 and relations to health and health behavior. *International Journal of Circumpolar Health, 65*(4), 305–12.

Stewart, S. E. (2007). *Concordance between teacher and student reports of physical and indirect bullying.* Unpublished thesis, University of Calgary, Canada.

Wheeler, E. (2004). Confronting social exclusion and bullying. *Childhood Education, 81*(1), 32L.

③

VICTIMS

Fact #21 Children are bullied and teased for different reasons! (Aluedse, 2006)

Gaining the Peaceful Edge . . . While there seem to be profiles of victims, bear in mind that in an instant, over the most incidental circumstances, anyone can become a victim of bullying.

Children may be victimized based on their physical appearance, such as weight or build, for being quiet or passive, or for standing out among their peers for whatever reason, even in a positive manner. Children are also bullied because of their social status.

In this context, bullies often isolate or exclude peers. Students can become social outcasts, and that image can perpetuate itself. Name-calling can also have long-term effects, and a name—good or bad—can stick sometimes into adulthood!

Children—boys in particular—who have difficulty in social situations tend to be more vulnerable to bullying. Often these children are hyperactive or have some emotional problems. This can affect their ability to make and maintain friendships.

In addition, those children who have special learning or physical needs are viewed as "different," along with those with a different sexual identity, who are also vulnerable to bullying.

However, it is important to recognize that while there are many factors that could make a student vulnerable to victimization, anyone can be a victim of bullying. Because there are so many factors that can impact a situation, adults must be vigilant in ensuring that a student is not being victimized, even if the student does not fit the common profile of a victim.

Fact #22 Adolescent confusion over what it means to be masculine is the root of homophobic bullying. (Kimmel & Mahler, 2003)

Gaining the Peaceful Edge . . . The prevalence of this homophobic bullying, teasing, and violence is shocking. According to a recent study in public schools in Massachusetts, 97 percent of high school students said they regularly hear homophobic remarks.

If you walk down a hallway in just about any middle school in the country, you will hear expressions such as "you fag." Any adolescent boy who exhibits any personality trait that can be viewed as weak or dependent can become a target of bullying. While these weaknesses are not unusual, boys often feel they need to show they are invulnerable, capable of anything, and fearless. It is a form of machismo—where boys define themselves by their perceived masculinity.

Young adolescent boys who demonstrate any personality traits other than independence and invulnerability are considered weak and may become targets for bullying. These weaknesses often threaten the fragile identities of their peers.

Girls also have certain stereotypical standards that define their behavior. If they display any characteristics that are not traditionally feminine, they are labeled as "dykes." This can be very hurtful and can cause social isolation.

It is very common for even adults to use homophobic language in their daily speech. We all have heard them—he is so "feminine" or he throws the ball like a girl. When adults use this language it gives tacit approval to students to imitate this behavior—and so the cycle continues.

Fact #23 Victims that are not aggressive when confronted with a bullying incident are known as passive victims. (Hanish & Guerra, 2004)

Gaining the Peaceful Edge . . . These are the children often viewed by their peers as weak and defenseless, making them more vulnerable to bullying experiences.

Students who are anxious, passive, and unassertive are more likely to be targeted by their peers. If they are boys, they tend to be called "feminine" names to challenge their masculine identity. They are viewed by their peers with distain.

What is even more frightening is that they are often disliked or in general disdained by the adults in their lives. There can be a common attitude that because they are not assertive, they "ask for it."

There is a certain attitude that these students deserve the ill treatment they receive or that they need to learn to defend themselves. There are even bullying prevention programs that claim that the key to bullying-prevention is to train students to stand up for themselves.

The reality is that the victim is not the problem. Bullying is a question of human rights—that everyone has the right to feel safe. Bullying is about an imbalance of power. If a student is being victimized because of an anxious or passive demeanor, he or she should not have to change to fit in with his/her peers.

Victims need our support and encouragement. Rather, it is the peers that need to be trained to be more accepting and empathic toward these students. When working toward a bully-free environment, we need to first protect the victims.

Fact #24 Sibling violence is another form of victimization. (Finkelhor, Turner, & Ormrod, 2006)

Gaining the Peaceful Edge . . . Bullying among siblings is a serious issue and a predictor of other bullying behaviors.

Today when a child reports that an older sibling is regularly hurting them we must take it seriously. Not only can this be a prelude to other forms of violence for the bully, but it can also cause long-term consequences for the victim.

Until recently we considered peer-on-peer violence as relatively benign because it is common and developmentally normal and there is no intent to inflict serious harm. It is simply dismissed as part of growing up. However, this being said, peer-on-peer violence should never be dismissed as kids' stuff.

When a victim has constant close contact with an attacker whose harassment goes unchecked, the violence escalates. This is what happens with siblings. There are assumptions that it is a common childhood phenomenon that does not have any serious consequences; however, recent research indicates that when bullying and victimization occurs between siblings, the consequences are as serious as the trauma symptoms from other forms of chronic victimization. Sibling bullying most commonly involves younger children between the ages of two and nine. Children in these situations report being hit and assaulted with an object, causing a bruise, a cut that bled, or a broken bone.

This tells us that we must take sibling bullying seriously and protect the victim, particularly when the victim is very young. Parents need to carefully listen to their children and watch for patterns of complaints that signal sibling bullying.

Fact #25 Victims need our help! (Kevorkian, 2006)

Gaining the Peaceful Edge . . . We can give students the support and protection that they need to overcome bullying experiences.

There are some key things that we can do to protect children from chronic bullying and victimization. However, it is important to remember, when we are talking about unequal power, which is one of the defining factors of a bullying situation, the responsibility should never be on the victim to solve the problem. We should:

- Listen to their story!
- Get all the facts and document everything.
- Show the child how to stay calm and not react to the bully. Sometimes when the bully does not get a reaction, they will stop—at least temporarily. This will give you as the adult time to appropriately assist the child.
- Give the child the message that it is their school, they belong there, and the problem is not their fault.
- Find out the school's policy on bullying. If there is none, developing a policy with the school is something very important to pursue in the future.
- Contact the teacher and plan a meeting to discuss the bullying concerns.
- Present all the documented information with names and dates to the school. Begin with the teacher, and then go to the school administration if the problem does not stop immediately.
- Ask for an investigation—and set a certain time (usually within a week) to review the results.
- Ask about measures to protect the victim from retaliation during this time and into the future.
- Check in with the child to be certain that there are no reoccurrences of the bullying.

Fact #26 Bully-victims are students who can be both a bully and a victim. (Holt, Finkelhor, & Kantor, 2007)

Gaining the Peaceful Edge . . . Bully-victims are students who are both a bully and a victim. They often have been victimized and then revert to inflicting the same behavior on others.

Although there is a tendency to categorize bullying into bullies, victims, and bystanders, we must realize that students may be a victim in a given circumstance and a bully in another circumstance. Sometimes when a bullied student is otherwise unable to stop the bullying, the victim may in turn exhibit those bullying behaviors to others.

These children learn that the misuse of power can be a means to get needs met. So the child will be inclined to victimize students who are younger or more vulnerable than themselves. They may also pick on their younger siblings. This is particularly true when there are little or no consequences for bullying behavior.

Because they have been victimized, bully-victims feel a sense of entitlement to perpetuate the behavior, particularly when there are no consistent consequences for bullying. We must send the message that bullying is never okay, even in retaliation or self-defense.

Bullying prevention requires a culture change for our children. It is difficult to identify a child who is involved in both roles. But it is important to make it clear that any form of bullying is unacceptable; a lack of action plays an integral part of the continuing behavior. We must help them recognize that making fun, excluding, and hurting others is bad manners, wrong, and will never be tolerated. Then the victims will feel supported and be less likely to take up bullying behaviors as a way to manage their abuse.

Fact #27 Bully-victims and bullies tend to have poor attitudes toward school and tend to be involved in more negative behaviors—including delinquency, weapons possession, and substance abuse. (Thunfors, 2007)

Gaining the Peaceful Edge . . . Boys who are both a bully and a victim are at the greatest risk for many psychosocial problems.

Children gain their love of learning from their early experiences in school. When children bully others, they often haven't received positive attention regarding behaviors that encourage learning and academic achievement. When students don't get recognized for positive behaviors, they will often seek out attention in any form, even negative. As these negative behaviors increase, academics often suffer.

There are some children who on occasion can behave both as a bully and as a victim. These children tend to have behavioral disorders and have difficulty in social situations. These children are often viewed by the adults in their lives as "asking" for the trouble they seem to encounter.

Children that exhibit bullying behaviors may also not develop healthy friendships, which are important to school age children. Children often see themselves in their peers. Those children who instill fear and humiliation may not receive genuine acts of kindness and friendship, thus not developing their empathy and social skills. This lack of empathy places them at risk for participation in delinquent behaviors, including, but not limited to, truancy, drugs, and alcohol abuse.

Fact #28 In some places, being a nerd is like a having communicable disease. (Bellmore, Witkow, Graham, & Juvonen, 2004)

Gaining the Peaceful Edge . . . Social norms dictate with whom students feel comfortable socializing and being seen with in public. Adolescents are on a perpetual quest to be cool, and there are strict social norms of acceptance by the group.

When we allow a culture that supports student exclusion and the development of social cliques, bullying behaviors become the norm. These factions use their power to set the tone of who is cool and who is not. This is an arena of exclusivity and isolation. If we want to stop victimization of students, we need to change school culture and prioritize respect for self and others. We must promote tolerance and encourage empathy. Children need to understand that making fun of someone else is never acceptable and will not be tolerated.

Student culture is critical to student success. Making fun of "nerds" and "freaks" can be very harmful to our youth. Kids don't really understand that they are hurting another person, sometimes to the point of depression or even worse. Building a positive culture is done over time by supporting prosocial behavior and consistently applying consequences for negative behavior.

Bullying in the context of fun cannot be dismissed as joking. When we ask groups of students why they pick on others, they say they don't pick on others but are just kidding around. If they really understood that they were causing emotional distress, they would discontinue or reduce the bullying behavior, and, in time, the entire climate would change.

Fact #29 Students who fight back are more likely to be victimized. (Bellmore et al., 2004)

Gaining the Peaceful Edge . . . The cycle of bullying and victimization is reinforced when the victim responds aggressively. This is contradictory to the notion that students should "stand up" for themselves.

Violence is never a good response to violence. It only escalates the situation. We should not tell students that they should fight back against bullies. In fact, we have found that standing up to the bully actually may increase victimization. One of the key factors in determining if a situation is bullying is the imbalance of power. This means that the bully has power over the victim, who simply cannot protect him- or herself. It is not a level playing field.

Mediation between the bully and the victim is not possible. In a true case of bullying, putting them together to work out their problems would simply revictimize the victim. Therefore, just as we would never tell a victim of a violent crime to stand up to the perpetrator, likewise we cannot expect victims of bullying to protect themselves.

Often the victim does not want to face the bully, because it is very likely that this will aggravate the situation. Everyone must understand bullying and the best practices for dealing with situations. This means having the right responses and reactions to assist the victim. We must protect victims so that we send the message that if you seek our help, we will support and help you. In a school where all adults recognize bullying, where there is a clear bullying prevention policy, and where there is a procedure for investigating incidents and clear consequences for the behavior, students who are victimized can feel safe.

Fact #30 Victims tend to lack social skills and blame themselves when they are bullied. (Christie, 2005)

Gaining the Peaceful Edge . . . Students who may be vulnerable to bullying can be identified before their problems escalate into serious situations.

Children are not born with social skills but must learn them through example and experiences. Social skills must be nurtured, just like academic skills such as reading and math. We must practice them, role-play, and go over scenarios to help our children understand what is acceptable and what is not.

Too often, children who are victimized blame themselves and don't understand that the bully is wrong. They often feel they deserve to be treated poorly by their peers, and their self-worth dwindles. We must help children understand behaviors that should neither be exhibited nor tolerated. Every child in a school, on a team, or in an organization has the right to be there and deserves an environment that encourages a sense of belonging and security. They should clearly be able to identify when someone is treating them unfairly and know how to respond. They need to know an adult they can trust to act appropriately and give them the assistance they need.

We must create a culture that promotes the social skills that help children model behaviors that promote healthy positive relationships. As adults, we must teach respect for self and others by giving it and receiving it. Parents must understand their role in promoting social skills to help their child gain a sense of belonging and a positive self-image. It is essential to realize that although many victims have poor social skills, anyone at any time can be victimized.

Fact #31 When asked, most middle school students said they would prefer to be athletic, popular, and nonstudious. When asked what they would least like to be, the response was nonathletic, unpopular, and studious. (Bishop, et al., 2004)

Gaining the Peaceful Edge . . . These strong cultural norms are an explanation of why bullying is so prevalent in middle school. Students have a very narrow view of what is acceptable, and anyone outside of those boundaries is at risk for becoming a victim of bullying.

Globally, athletes are recognized and celebrated for their skills and winning seasons. Children learn early on that if you want to be cool, rich, and successful, you should become an athlete. Someone who studies and puts forth their best effort in school is usually not voted the prom king or queen. The studious student is usually called a nerd or bookworm. It is highly likely you will see a football or basketball player hanging on a teen's wall and not a picture of Einstein or a Nobel Peace Prize winner. We have set a culture globally that says brains and popularity never go hand in hand, and now we have the tough job of removing that stereotype.

This narrow view of what is acceptable doesn't promote in our youth the characteristics that should be sought after and celebrated. How can we reduce bullying in schools if we don't help change the view our kids have of success? When will saving lives though research breakthroughs become a desired trait? How will we gain the "buy in" from schools and communities to help change perceptions of what is popular and successful? We must help spread a new epidemic that imbues people who display acts of kindness and wisdom with the same excitement as the winning quarterback. When this occurs, we will start to see high-achieving students with exemplary service have both high ranks in GPA and among their peers.

REFERENCES

Aluedse, O. (2006). Bullying in schools: A form of child abuse in schools. *Educational Research Quarterly*, 30(1), 37.

Bellmore, A., Witkow, M., Graham, S., & Juvonen, J. (2004). Beyond the individual: The impact of ethnic context and classroom behavioral norms on victims' adjustment. *Developmental Psychology*, 40(6), 1,159.

Bishop, J. H., Bishop, M., Bishop, M., Gelbwasser, L., Green, S., Peterson, E., Rubinsztaj, A., & Zuckerman, A. (2004). Why we harass nerds and freaks: A formal theory of student culture and norms. *Journal of School Health*, 74(7), 235.

Boyle, D. J. (2005). Youth bullying: Incidence, impact, and interventions. *Journal of the New Jersey Psychological Association*, 55(3), 22.

Christie, K. (2005). Chasing the bullies away. *Phi Delta Kappan*, 86(10), 725.

Finkelhor, D., Turner, H., & Ormrod, R. (2006). Kid's stuff: The nature and impact of peer and sibling violence on younger and older children. *Child Abuse & Neglect*, 30(12), 1,401.

Hanish, L., & Guerra, N. (2004). Aggressive victims, passive victims, and bullies: Developmental continuity or developmental change? *Merrill-Palmer Quarterly*, 50(1), 17.

Holt, M., Finkelhor, D., & Kantor, G. K. (2007). Hidden forms of victimization in elementary students involved in bullying. *School Psychology Review*, 36(3), 345.

Kevorkian, M. (2006). *Preventing bullying: Helping kids form positive relationships*. Lanham, MD: Rowman & Littlefield Education.

Kimmel, M., & Mahler, M. (2003). Adolescent masculinity, homophobia, and violence: Random school shootings, 1982–2001. *American Behavioral Scientist*, 46(10), 20.

Thunfors, P. (2007). *The distinguishing characteristics of a popular subtype of bully*. Unpublished diss., University of Virginia.

4

BULLIES

Fact #32 Bullies tend to lack empathy for their victims. (Ward 2007)

Gaining the Peaceful Edge . . . Teaching kids to care for one another is key to preventing bullying.

There are many common characteristics of a student who is likely to bully. But one common denominator is lack of empathy. Children who use bullying behavior tend not to have sympathy or compassion for their peers. When children who bully have no concept of the pain that they are imposing on another child, they are more likely to continue or even escalate the bullying.

This is especially true with cyberbullying. Because the bullying takes place in an anonymous atmosphere, it is easy to not have empathy for the victim. The bully does not have to face the victim, and consequently they do not have to confront the devastation the bullying causes. There is evidence that in the electronic arena, the bullying is much worse because of the anonymity.

Because of the Internet, in an instant, personal communications can become vastly public—in an instant, everyone at school can have access to private and potentially embarrassing information. Even worse, rumors, innuendos, or lies can be made public without the victim ever knowing who is responsible for the vicious slander or hurtful insults. All of this can happen without the perpetrators ever having to face their victim. They do not have to face the consequence of personally witnessing the devastating effect of their cyber actions.

Contrary to the myth that bullies bully because they do not feel good about themselves, research shows that they tend to have strong psychological profiles and enjoy social popularity. Their popularity gives them more confidence and the power to bully others without facing social consequences for their behavior.

Therefore the need to develop empathy with all students becomes even more important. They need to understand that all forms of bullying can be very hurtful. By focusing on the impact on the victims and developing empathy, students are more likely to refrain from bullying behavior.

Fact #33 Adolescents who bully often are popular and psychologically strong. (Thunfors, 2007)

Gaining the Peaceful Edge . . . Don't be fooled by the popular student who uses power as a negative way to gain control over peers—because that is bullying behavior.

When asked what a bully looks like, most students will describe someone who is mean, sinister, and threatening, looming over their victims. It is as if there were an evil person lurking in the shadows of the halls and school grounds waiting to humiliate and destroy their victims. But despite these perceptions, the reality is that the popular kids are very likely to use their popularity in a negative way.

They will use their status within a group to humiliate others. Because they tend to be psychologically stronger than their peers, they use that ability to control others. This means that bullies can enjoy high social status. Ironically, because these bullies have high social status they tend to become even stronger psychologically. Other kids recognize this, and even though the bully may be popular, others will avoid them. They simply do not want to become a target of the bullying.

In the long run, this means that those who are both bullied and victimized are all negatively impacted by this behavior. Students who are stressed from these conditions will display inappropriate behavior and other types of antisocial behavior. This can include being withdrawn, detached, or exceedingly angry and aggressive.

All of these factors are most prominent during early adolescence. That means that the combination of physical development and the myriad feelings that accompany adolescence collide with social issues in middle school. This is when the issues of peer connection and social status are most important to the child. We have learned through developmental research that social status is one of the strongest predictors of high self-esteem and emotional well-being. Therefore we know that bullies, because of their popularity, do not feel depressed, anxious, or lonely.

But it is important to note that the peers that surround the bully are usually there because of the social connection, fear of becoming a target, or even because they are bullies themselves. This tells us that fear can be an integral part of social status.

The high social status of bullies can be a particular challenge for adults when dealing with bullying problems. For most adults it is hard to believe that the most popular child is the bully. This emphasizes the importance of systemic programs to solve the problem of bullying.

Fact #34 Bullies are more likely to engage in vandalism, shoplifting, truancy, and substance abuse than students who do not bully during early childhood. (Sourander et al., 2007)

Gaining the Peaceful Edge . . . Understand that bullying can be a prelude to more serious forms of violent behavior.

The evidence is clear and overwhelming that bullies, when allowed to continue, will escalate the behavior as they get older. Vandalism, shoplifting, and truancy are all destructive aggressive behaviors. There is also a direct correlation between substance abuse and gun violence and bullying behavior. Kids do not begin at that level; they often have had considerable experience with other types of antagonistic behaviors.

Think of the school yard as a learning laboratory for social behaviors. This is where kids get to practice different roles. They are learning to define themselves and to understand their position in their small social environment.

When a child is allowed to continue to use aggressive and hurtful behavior, they simply get better at it. This can include relational bullying. This behavior then grows into more serious versions of the same. For instance, relational violence can grow into other types of abuse, including dating violence and spousal abuse.

When put into this context, it drives home the importance of dealing with this behavior long before there are more victims with much more serious consequences. When it continues unchecked after the age of seven, the ability to make a change for the better is more difficult. The good news is that when there is consistent and appropriate intervention, bullying behavior can be reversed.

Fact #35 Overly aggressive and overly permissive parents are equally likely to have children who bully.

Gaining the Peaceful Edge . . . Parenting can be an important influence on children and their attitudes toward bullying.

The aggressive pattern of bullying can begin at home. Parents that are very negative, are critical, and lack warmth increase the possibility of raising children who bully. Empathy is aparamount to bullying prevention, and children begin learning about it at a very early age within the home environment.

We know that children model their behavior by observing people around them. Parents who are overly punitive and harsh are sending their children the message that this is the appropriate way to respond to others around them. Similarly, parents who use physical forms of punishment are fostering the notion that violence produces violence. In other words, it is okay to respond to hitting by hitting back. Instead, it is important to set clear rules and to impose consequences when the rules are broken. But these consequences should not include hitting, because it teaches nothing other than that it is okay to hit.

There are also clear messages about the use of power in this type of parenting that are being sent to the child. Through overly strict and harsh discipline, we are teaching children that power can be used in a punitive way to get their needs met.

On the other hand, parents who are overly permissive can also be at risk for encouraging kids to bully others. These parents do not apply consequences for aggressive behavior. They tend to excuse the behavior because of "extenuating" circumstances. They offer children excuses and allow the behavior to continue. In other situations they may simply allow the behavior to continue, expecting the consequences to come from the environment. In other words—there is a parental attitude that sooner or later the child will run into someone who is bigger and stronger who will hit them harder.

Children need structure, positive discipline that teaches empathy, caring, and reasonable and consistent consequences when the rules are broken.

Fact #36 There are clear indicators that even children with high self-esteem can be bullies. (Baumeister, Campbell, Krueger, & Vohs, 2003)

Gaining the Peaceful Edge . . . We cannot judge a student by how they feel about themselves; we have to look at their behavior.

This is one of the most difficult myths about bullying to overcome. Research indicates that self-esteem seems to be an indicator of intensified prosocial and antisocial tendencies. High self-esteem can mean that a student can be either a positive or negative leader. In other words, we cannot assume that a student who thinks well of him/herself is not a bully, because he/she can use that self confidence either to bully or to defend victims.

It is extremely important to note that just as anyone can be a victim, anyone can use bullying behaviors. We cannot make judgments solely based in self-esteem. We need to look at behavior. While there are many circumstances that can influence a child's behavior, there are some specific signs that the student may be engaging in bullying behavior.

Bullies tend to incessantly tease, call names, or ridicule other students. They are free with threats and intimidation. This behavior is usually directed toward students who are weaker and relatively defenseless. Bullies may also encourage or demand that their peers bully others on their behalf. Girls who bully typically are more likely to manipulate relationships, pass rumors, or even lie about the victim.

General speaking, bullies tend to be bigger, stronger, older, smarter, or have social advantages over their victim. They tend to have a need to dominate and can be hot tempered. Characteristically, bullies have difficulty conforming to rules and may be impulsive. They can frustrate easily and are often defiant and oppositional and are aggressive toward adults. Most importantly, they have little or no empathy toward others.

All of these behaviors are red flags, and adults should closely watch students who behave in this manner. However, we cannot assume that these are the only bullies in our midst. Some are very popular and likewise clever. We need to be diligent and think in terms of protecting all students from all types of bullies.

Fact #37 Bullying behaviors are learned. (Berger, 2007)

Gaining the Peaceful Edge . . . The sooner we act, the better the chances we can stop bullying behavior.

Children and teens who exhibit bullying behaviors sometimes say they are just joking around. They are modeling what they see in real life and the media. They don't understand that their behavior can have a long-lasting impact on the children around them. Adults unintentionally reinforce bullying behaviors by responding to children in inappropriate ways. Using coercion, power, and demeaning tactics to maintain a classroom or household are ways we may serve as poor role models for bullying prevention. This negative form of communication actually becomes the example for the child to mimic. Sometimes as adults we don't realize that our behavior is teaching our children how to respond to and communicate with others.

When raising children we must act like the adults we are hoping our children will become. We must take positive role modeling seriously in order to be sure that we are not passing on destructive social skills, which are not only damaging to the child but are also a part of a continuing cycle of poor child rearing and educative practices. In an environment where a negative behavior is not monitored or stopped, the behavior will flourish. We can help reduce the number of bullies by not fostering, teaching, and modeling bullying behavior.

Bullying is a learned behavior; the fact remains that if it is allowed to continue it will escalate. As long as the bully gets his/her needs met, the behavior will continue. There is no incentive to stop. It becomes peer abuse and a part of the continuum of interpersonal violence. It is up to us as parents and teachers to stop the cycle.

Fact #38 A lack of adult intervention reinforces bullying. (Bradshaw, Sawyer, & O'Brennan, 2007)

Gaining the Peaceful Edge . . . As adults, we must sharpen our knowledge and awareness of bullying incidents so we can be ready to protect children from victimization.

Responding swiftly and appropriately to bullying behavior is crucial. Currently, research supports the idea that bullying behaviors in children most often continue without any action or consequence from adults. In fact, kids report that adults only respond two out of every ten times they report that they have been bullied. Sometimes the adult does not recognize the seriousness of the bullying behavior, while other times the adult simply may choose to not respond. Regardless of the reason, silence encourages the tormenter.

When our kids notice that an adult does not do anything to correct a certain behavior, they easily come to the conclusion that the behavior must be okay. In the past, we believed that telling the child to handle the behavior themselves developed self-reliance. This reinforces the wrong idea that bullying is a normal part of life and that kids must learn how to handle it.

There are many reasons why adults may not respond to a bullying situation. Sometimes it is because they simply do not know when it happens. The average bullying incident takes only thirty-seven seconds. In that time a child can be victimized without our even being aware that anything has happened.

Adults may simply be too busy to handle a bullying situation. When asked, adults say they always respond to physical bullying but often do not feel it necessary to intervene when the bullying is verbal. The reality is that verbal aggression often escalates, and by stopping it when it is verbal, you are preventing a potential physical situation.

Fact #39 Bullies do not see what they are doing as wrong. (Rallis, Rossman, Cobb, Reagan, &Kuntz, 2007)

Gaining the Peaceful Edge . . . Clear rules and consistent conse-quences about bullying behavior are crucial to making kids feel safe at home and in school.

The lack of policies and rules regarding bullying contributes to the ever-growing population of bullies. In life there are certain things that we know are not acceptable and will not go unaddressed. When kids reach driving age and study for the test, they learn that failing to stop at a stop sign or speeding will result in costly tickets and that repeated offenses may result in loss of driving privileges. There are clear rules and consequences when the rules are broken.

However, when it comes to bullying, there are no clear rules. Chil-dren and teens easily recognize that the monitoring and consequences for bullying behavior vary from adult to adult. To reduce the number of bullies, adults must make bullying prevention a priority. Laws, poli-cies, and rules must exist to provide the groundwork for careful mon-itoring and informing parents of cases regarding bullying. We need a clear definition of bullying so that all stakeholders, teachers, parents, students, and other adults recognize bullying when they see it.

Additionally, they must understand how to apply appropriate con-sequences. The consequences need to be consistent, and everyone needs to understand that they will be held accountable for their ac-tions. It will take time, but when kids know what to expect for nega-tive bullying behavior, the environment will change for the better. It also sends a message to the victim that they do not have to accept the cruelty of the bully.

Fact #40 Bullies may believe that bullying fosters respect. (Taylor, 2007)

Gaining the Peaceful Edge . . . Don't be fooled by the popular student, because popularity can be a platform for bullying that can hurt or ostracize others.

Bullies usually travel in groups. Some kids follow the bully who they think most popular. Sometimes children participate in these groups because they need to have a sense of belonging. But more often it is because they are afraid of the bully.

These bully leaders think that they are respected because of the group that follows them around. Many times, these kids don't realize the hurt they are causing others. Kids need acceptance, and we as adults must help them feel like they belong. Kids use making fun of others to get attention and laughs out of their peers. These bullies may lack a sense of who they are and a sense of how to treat others. They may think that exhibiting bullying behaviors will prevent them from being left out or being bullied themselves.

When bullying behavior brings a student to the center of a group, it is because of a misuse of power rooted in social status, age, or physical dominance. When asked to describe a bully, the description given closely parallels that of the most popular student. The difference is that a leader uses the power to help, support, and include others, while the bully does the opposite, which can be frightening to followers and devastating to others. Most importantly, when bystanders observe this behavior, they learn that bullying is a means to attain popularity and other social gains. Unchecked, the bullying perpetuates negative behavior.

Fact #41 Bullies need to have parent involvement to minimize their behavior. (Stevens, De Bourdeaudhuij, & Van Oost, 2002)

Gaining the Peaceful Edge . . . Parents are on the front line to recognize and deter bullying behavior.

Parent involvement is necessary to help children succeed. In order for us to help children who are exhibiting bullying behaviors, parents must recognize this conduct in their children. This can be very difficult because parents often don't want to see some of the negative things their child may be doing. They may rationalize negative behaviors they see in their children by thinking that it is only a phase.

But it is important for parents to be vigilant when they suspect their child is bullying others. Sometimes this can be manifested in actions between siblings. There are telltale signs of broken or missing toys or unexplained bruises that can be indicators of a more serious pattern of behavior. It is up to the parent to investigate these occurrences before they escalate or get carried into the school setting.

As children grow up they also keep many secrets from their parents. Just as children do not want to readily admit they are afraid of someone at school, kids are not forthcoming about bullying behaviors they inflict on their peers. Sometimes the approval of adults, especially parents, makes kids think that making fun of some groups of people is okay. We tend to see this against the gay and lesbian community. This is also reinforced in bigotry against people by race, gender, or religion. Joking and stereotyping groups of people sends the message that making fun of certain folks is okay. Bullies don't feel the pain they cause in their victims. Bullies need to learn tolerance and become sensitive to others' feelings.

REFERENCES

Baumeister, R. F., Campbell, J. D., Krueger, J. I., & Vohs, K. D. (2003). Does high self-esteem cause better performance, interpersonal success, happiness, or healthier lifestyles? *Psychological Science in the Public Interest*, *4*(1), 1.

Berger, K. (2007). Update on bullying at school: Science forgotten? *Developmental Review*, *27*, 90.

Bradshaw, C., Sawyer, A., & O'Brennan, L. (2007). Bullying and peer victimization at school: Perceptual differences between students and school staff. School *Psychology Review*, *36*(3), 361.

Rallis, S., Rossman, G., Cobb, C., Reagan, T., & Kuntz, A. (2007). *Leading dynamic schools: How to create and implement ethical policies.* Thousand Oaks, CA: Corwin Press.

Sourander, A., Jensen, P., Ronning, J. A., Elonheimo, H., Niemela, S., Helenius, H., et al. (2007). Childhood bullies and victims and their risk of criminality in late adolescence: The Finnish "From a Boy to a Man" study. *Archives of Pediatric and Adolescent Medicine*, *161*(6), 546.

Stevens, V., De Bourdeaudhuij, I., & Van Oost, P. (2002). Relationship of the family environment to children's involvement in bully/victim problems at school. *Journal of Youth and Adolescence*, *31*(6), 419.

Taylor, R. J. (2007). *An evaluation of owning up: Impact on perceptions of relational aggression, bullying, and victimization.* Unpublished diss., Hofstra University, New York.

Thunfors, P. (2007). *The distinguishing characteristics of a popular subtype of bully.* Unpublished diss., University of Virginia.

Ward, S. K. (2007). *Patterns of discrete social skills among incarcerated middle school youth with bullying and victimization problems.* Unpublished Ph.D. diss., University of Illinois at Urbana-Champaign, United States—Illinois.

5

BYSTANDERS

Fact #42 Elementary school children who witness bullying are at risk for long-term troublesome and depressive behaviors. (Snyder et al., 2003)

Gaining the Peaceful Edge . . . Bullying at any age is unacceptable, but we must be particularly aware of these behaviors in young children.

The research clearly indicates that children as young as five years who continually observe bullying that goes on unchecked or ignored by adults are at greater risk of becoming bullies themselves. It is hard to believe that young children can use bullying behavior, and many people see bullying as a problem in only middle school and high school. Not understanding that bullying can begin at a very young age hinders prevention and intervention efforts with this vulnerable group.

By continually observing bullying behavior that has no consequences and little to no adult intervention, children may become nervous, fearful, and uncomfortable at school. These reactions and negative responses may foster a feeling of helplessness or insecurity that can lead to depression in later years. All children are exposed to bullying—

either as a bully, victim, or a bystander, and most of the time this goes unaddressed by adults. The good news is that when bullying behavior is checked in children younger than the age of eight, it is easier to reverse these tendencies and reduce future instances of bullying as these children get older.

Research supports that adults intervene less than 5 percent of the time bullying occurs. This sends the message to children that bullying is a reality and is here to stay. Additionally, from a child's perspective, there is no need to tell an adult because they can't or choose not to help. Children should be confident and comfortable in their surroundings. The violence and cruelty associated with bullying should not become a regular part of a child's school day. We can do this by providing an atmosphere where respect and appreciation for others is nurtured and corrective action is consistently taken when bullying does occur.

Fact #43 Witnessing repetitive abuse in the form of bullying has measurable long-term effects on bystanders. (Bonanno, 2007)

Gaining the Peaceful Edge . . . When dealing with bullying, it is important to understand that this destructive behavior seriously impacts bystanders.

Recently, secondhand smoking has been linked to serious health issues including, but not limited to, lung cancer. As a result, many public places do not allow smoking, and laws have become stringent to protect citizens from the dangers of secondhand smoke.

In a like manner, when we think about the dangers of our children's exposure to bullying behaviors day in and day out, before, during, and after school, as well as in the virtual world, we must be concerned about the long-term effects it may have on those that witness bullying—the bystanders.

Of course, the victim suffers considerably from bullying, but we now know that bullying seriously impacts the bystanders as well as the bully and the victim. The bystander experiences both a physical and emotional reaction to repeated exposure to bullying. We have learned that this causes stress, anxiety, apprehension, and other types of physical responses in children.

Therefore we must focus our efforts on empowering bystanders and protecting them from overexposure. When talking with children about bullying incidents, it is important to include the bystander in the discussion of feelings and what could be done to interrupt the bullying.

Fact #44 The role of peer bystanders is crucial in reducing bullying. (Lodge & Frydenberg, 2005)

Gaining the Peaceful Edge . . . You can help children by talking to them about safe ways in which they can help the victim in a bullying situation.

Teaching students how to respond to bullying situations can be crucial in reducing bullying. Many students express concern for the victim but do not get involved. They may often actively participate, passively watch, or ignore the situation entirely. We must encourage our young people to stand up for what is right.

This should be something each child puts into practice in all aspects of their life, including when they witness bullying to one of their peers. Not every child can go up to a bully and say "stop it" or "knock it off." However, they can walk away and refuse to be a passive bystander who gives the bullying an audience. If we have the belief that adults can and will do something, we can encourage reporting to the nearest adult. Sometimes when the child exhibiting the bullying behaviors does not have an audience or feel that they are acting cool in front of their friends, the behavior will decline. We have all heard the expression that "there is safety in numbers."

Peer bystanders can invite a child who has been victimized or targeted to walk with them or sit with them at lunch instead of isolating them, as we see so often when a child has been victimized. In regards to cyber-bullying, peer bystanders can send a message by not forwarding or responding to nasty e-mails. We must challenge children to find their comfort level and learn how valuable their role and their actions are in bullying prevention.

Our children are faced with a dilemma of when to tell an adult because to them tattling or telling on someone is worse than most actions, including failing school and cheating. It is important that children know that helping out a peer in need and getting an adult when necessary is how you keep your friends and school safe. When you tell an adult something and your intention is to keep your friends safe, that is reporting. When you tell an adult something to get your friend in trouble, then you are tattling and that is certainly not what we are encouraging. We must also communicate that all reporting is confidential. Once this is established and children know it to be true, it is highly likely the incidents of reporting will increase.

Fact #45 Bystanders who view verbal bullying often feel uncomfortable. (Lodge & Frydenberg, 2005)

Gaining the Peaceful Edge . . . You can help bystanders by talking to them about recognizing that they have the power to eliminate bullying by simply speaking up for the victim.

Generally speaking, bystanders feel uncomfortable with the verbal bullying that they witness. They have expressed disgust and anger toward the bully. Girls tend to feel troubled, sad, and even angry. For girls, the social context of their lives is paramount, so verbal bullying can be devastating. Boys, on the other hand, most often feel indifferent when they witness bullying behavior.

Both boys and girls have conflicted feelings about verbal bullying. They report feeling guilty and angry and fear that at the slightest provocation, they too can become the target of the bullying. This becomes the most important reason why kids allow and even encourage the bullying behavior. Simply stated, most kids would rather remain silent or even participate in bullying rather than take steps to prevent it because they fear they could be next!

It is really important to help these bystanders by talking to them about some appropriate responses or ways to help the victim. The best way is through a schoolwide bullying-prevention program. When these programs are in place, the entire school is charged with the responsibility of supporting the victim. However, kids can be taught to help the victim though a variety of ways.

The bystander can interrupt the bullying by helping the victim to leave the situation. Humor is also a good tactic to diffuse a situation, or, most importantly, the bystander can go to an adult to help. When it becomes fashionable for bystanders to intervene—and this happens regularly—the bullying will decrease dramatically.

Fact #46 Often kids who watch while a peer is being bullied feel un-comfortable—because they feel it is wrong and they do not know how to respond. (Jeffrey, 2004)

Gaining the Peaceful Edge . . . It is an indication of a sense of social responsibility when children feel uncomfortable as they see others being bullied.

Our children have realized that bullying is prevalent in our schools and worry that they too can become a victim at any time or in any place. This fear may dissuade children who want to help from taking any sort of action to assist. A child once commented, "If my mom can't help and my teacher can't help, what can I do to stop the bullying?"

We must minimize the risk associated with bystander action by educating all stakeholders with children on ways they can help the victim. We need to show them that bystanders, not just bullies, can have power too.

This can be done by having conversations with children from the earliest age about how we all need to protect each other. This helps develop social awareness and consciousness. We can stress the importance of taking care of our friends. In addition, we need to reward children who speak up for others.

This reinforces the value of caring for one another. It shows that you are not only respecting their courage but you are supporting prosocial behavior. The reward can be as simple as a verbal acknowledgement: "Good job—I am proud of you for taking care of your friend."

Fact #47 Most of the time, bystanders do not respond because they are afraid. (Lodge & Frydenberg, 2005)

Gaining the Peaceful Edge . . . You can help bystanders by talking to them about safe ways to help a victim.

We have heard stories where people have witnessed crimes in action or people in distress and did nothing because they were afraid for a number of reasons. These same feelings are shared by many of our children, who feel uncomfortable while watching children being victimized but do not know the best way to respond. They have not been taught what to do when faced with a real-life situation.

These lessons on how to respond must come from the adults in their life, including parents and educators. Just as we foster conversations about what to do if somebody offers you drugs or if a stranger tries to solicit a child, we must have conversations and role-playing scenarios on how to respond and intervene in bullying situations.

First of all, you have to teach the child how to assess a situation to determine if it is safe for them to intervene. Not all circumstances are safe for a bystander to attempt to help a victim. If a child feels afraid that he/she could be hurt or could become a target of the bullying, he/she needs to know where they can go for help.

In addition, they need tips on how to ask for help. They need to be able to ask so that the adult will understand the situation, who is involved, and where it is happening. If the adult does not help out, we need to give children permission to go to another adult for help.

If the situation is safe and the child does not feel any apprehension about stepping into the situation, a simple "Hey, leave him alone" to the bully or "Let's get out of here" can be a good way to help the victim. The more we work with children, the more likely they will have the confidence to act and be a helpful bystander in a bullying situation.

Fact #48 Sometimes bystanders can be just as guilty as the bully because they support and encourage the bully by joining in and encouraging the behavior. (Coloroso, 2005)

Gaining the Peaceful Edge . . . It is important to recognize that not all bystanders are simply inadvertent observers of the bullying behavior.

Bystanders come in all shapes, sizes, attitudes, and levels of involvement. Think about the crowd that often forms when a child is being victimized. Some of those bystanders will actually encourage the bullying. They will laugh, leer, and call out to encourage the behavior. They may even join in the pushing, hitting, and other bullying activity.

These are the students who, given the opportunity, would initiate the bullying. They are watching and taking note of the power that the bully is exerting in that situation. They are the students most likely to bully themselves. They are primary contributors to the climate of fear and intimidation. Other students know that like the bully these students are potential perpetrators of the same bullying behavior.

There are also bystanders who will not actively participate but will stand around and watch. These students are there because perhaps they are enjoying the bullying, or they may even be grateful that they are not the victim. They would not initiate the bullying, but their presence is a form of participation. They are the source of the power that the bully gains from the behavior. The sense of intimidation runs powerful and deep, impacting everyone, and contributes to the long-term negative effect on bystanders.

There are also those that are neutral on the matter of bullying. They want to stay away and do not necessarily care one way or the other. They have no empathy for the victim. They have no feeling or opinion about the bully. They simply see it as none of their business. Many students fall into this category.

All of these bystanders need to understand their role in the cycle of the bullying behavior. Their presence and encouragement is a serious contributor. We need to develop empathy with these students. They need to understand the impact of the behavior on the victim. This, along with consequences for negative behavior, is the key to eliminating the bullying and creating a caring school climate.

Fact #49 When bystanders see that there are consequences for bullying behavior, they are less likely to participate in bullying. (MacNeil & Newell, 2004)

Gaining the Peaceful Edge . . . It is important to send a clear, consistent, and age-appropriate message that bullying is unacceptable.

In general, everyone needs to be aware of the consequences for bullying. They need to know that this is unacceptable and that there are clear consequences for the behavior. When intervening in these situations, these bystanders need to know that their participation is a fundamental part of the problem.

Most bullying takes place in groups. It is the presence of those bystanders that gives the bully the audience that heightens the victim's humiliation. Not only does the victim feel the pain of the bullying but he/she also feels the sting of being humiliated in front of peers.

It is important to help children recognize the difference between assertive and aggressive behavior. Assertiveness is the ability to speak up for oneself. For example, Peter was pushed hard by another student. A teacher overheard a bystander respond "Leave him alone!" Later she praised him for his assertiveness. He was making it crystal clear that the behavior was inappropriate. At that point the incident was over. Should it reoccur, the teacher would have to intervene.

When there are planned responses to bullying behavior, it takes the personal side out of the equation. When a school has rules for bullying and stated consequences for breaches of those rules, it makes dealing with the bully much easier. In other words, you can simply say to the student with a calm and even tone of voice, "We do not allow bullying here and since rules have been broken, this is the consequence." This is simple, impersonal, and direct.

To be effective, these consequences must be clear, consistent, logical, and nonviolent. In addition, consequences must be age-appropriate and should match the severity of the issue. This means that when considering the consequences all of these factors must be considered so the consequences will become a teaching discipline aimed at reducing the behavior.

Fact #50 Passive bystanders are those students who do not participate in the bullying but do not act to stop it. (Elfstrom, 2007)

Gaining the Peaceful Edge . . . It is important to recognize that some bystanders, with the right tools, will be able to intervene in bullying situations.

Some bystanders feel uncomfortable when witnessing bullying behavior. One of the reasons they may feel uncomfortable is because they do not know what to do. "I would like to help, because I think bullying is wrong." This student is already demonstrating one of the key components to eliminating bullying—empathy.

We can build on the empathy by providing these bystanders with the tools to help the victim. Ask the child what some possible options to help a victim might be. Most often the child will come up with a list that includes telling the bully to stop, asking an adult to help, getting the victim to leave, making a joke, and comforting the victim. All of these are viable solutions. What is important is that by brainstorming with the child about these options, the child will have an opportunity to think in advance about their course of action.

When they have a plan, bystanders who have empathy for the victim are more likely to intervene. The tools will give them the confidence to respond, knowing that it is not only the right thing but the right way.

When you notice on television or in a story a scene where a bystander appropriately intervenes, you can point this out to the child. There are many stories of courage—and adults can use those instances as teachable moments to discuss the courage it takes to be a support to a victim. This demonstrates your values and sends a powerful message about your expectations.

We must be aware of the level of courage it takes for a child to intervene. Just tell the bully to stop or go ask someone for help—it looks simple to us as adults but may be absolutely terrifying to a child. If you translate your request to the child into a situation that you as an adult may be confronted with, you will realize how tough it is to intervene in a bullying situation. How many adults would jump in if they saw a woman being bullied by a man in a public setting?

Therefore it is very important to talk to kids about assessing a situation according to their own personal safety. If they decide direct intervention would take more courage than they have, they need to know about ways in which they can involve an adult. Above all, we need to praise a child for exhibiting courage—that is the best way to reinforce this positive behavior.

Fact #51 When bystanders look out for their friends, bullying decreases, and the school climate improves. (Elfstrom, 2007)

Gaining the Peaceful Edge . . . Adults cannot see everything; therefore we need to rely on bystanders to help eliminate bullying.

The average incident of bullying takes thirty-seven seconds! Because of that, it is impossible to expect adults to witness and intervene in every single instance. Most children who have been surveyed say that a large percentage of the bullying takes place in the classroom—right in front of the teacher. We are not implying that teachers are bad—ineffective or negligent. Rather we are saying that bullying happens so quickly and regularly that it is impossible for adults to catch every single incident. In fact teachers tell us that they most often respond when the bullying becomes physical—therefore leaving scores of verbal and bullying gestures unnoticed.

Teaching kids friendship skills is key to decreasing bullying. Also when a child has good friends they are less likely to be singled out by a bully. Every child should have at least one good friend.

Kids need to be able to know the difference between a close friend (someone who they spend the majority of their time with and can trust with their personal secrets), a buddy (team mate), and an acquaintance (someone they see around their school). Making these distinctions is important to help the child determine whom they can trust.

As adults, we need to model friendship. Children learn by observing, so we need to be friendly while at the same time valuing our close friendships. We need to be the type of friend that we expect our child to be. Kids need to have good friends and understand the value of those friends. They are then much more likely to defend those friends in the face of conflict with a student who is using bullying behavior to inflict harm. This will in turn contribute to the reduction of bullying and improve the social climate.

REFERENCES

Bonanno, R. A. (2007). *Bullied to the brink: An investigation of students at risk for depression and suicidal ideation.* Unpublished diss., The University of British Columbia, Canada.

Coloroso, B. (2005). A bully's bystanders are never innocent. *The Education Digest, 70*(8), 49.

Elfstrom, J. L. (2007). *Bullying and victimization: School climate matters.* Unpublished thesis, Miami University, Ohio.

Jeffrey, L. (2004). Bullying bystanders. *The Prevention Researcher, 11*(3), 7.

Lodge, J., & Frydenberg, E. (2005). The role of peer bystanders in school bullying: Positive steps toward promoting peaceful schools. *Theory into Practice, 44*(4), 329.

MacNeil, G., & Newell, J. (2004). School bullying: Who, why, and what to do. *The Prevention Researcher, 11*(3), 15.

Snyder, J., Brooker, M., Patrick, M. R., Snyder, A., Schrepferman, L., & Stoolmiller, M. (2003). Observed peer victimization during early elementary school: Continuity, growth, and relation to risk for child antisocial and depressive behavior. *Child Development, 74*(6), 1,881.

6

CYBERBULLYING

Fact #52 Cyberbullying is a specific form of bullying. It is a deliberate and intentional act that happens through electronic means. (Strom & Strom, 2005)

Gaining the Peaceful Edge . . . Always monitor your child's Internet access, including e-mail and cell phone.

This is a relatively new form of bullying. With the introduction of electronic communication, kids have been able to expand the ways they can hurt one another. This can be done by sending cruel or threatening e-mails and text messages. Students can spread rumors online and set up websites that poke fun at someone.

There are chat rooms, blogs, and websites that are available to all who wish to participate. These can be filled with nontruths, damaging lies, personal information, and embarrassing secrets about a student. This information can be transmitted to an entire student body and beyond with a simple click of a button. The end results can be devastating.

The exposure often goes unchecked and can occur twenty-four hours a day, seven days a week. Cyberbullying can stem from innocent pictures and websites that are cut, pasted, and misused. Once the information is out there, whether it is true or not does not matter. Others can simply pick up on it and expand on it to even greater levels of cruelty. One parent said that once the cyberbullying started, it was picked up by other students and everyone joined in by adding their own malicious opinions and comments. Several times a day, the student received these e-mails and phone calls. It was positively demoralizing.

When the victim is not in front of them, kids seem to become much braver and willing to send or forward mean messages. Often kids will say that they had no idea they were causing so much pain, even though they know that saying hurtful things about someone is wrong.

Perpetrators do not usually have to face the consequences that they may in a personal encounter due to very little reporting of cyberbullying incidences. Children often fear that reporting cyberbullying may result in a reduction or removal of Internet privileges. This fear often causes children to suffer in silence and not seek adult assistance.

Fact #53 Cell phones can be an instant way of reporting bullying incidents. (Beale & Hall, 2007)

Gaining the Peaceful Edge . . . Parents need to consider with whom and when their child is using their cell phone.

Specifically, parents can see from most cell phone bills the details about phone calls and text messaging that happened during a billing period. While we believe that children should have privacy, we as parents have a duty to be certain that the child is using their cell phone responsibly. Adults, especially parents, must be familiar with the features, such as pictures and instant messaging, on the phones they purchase for their children. You should not give your child a phone that you don't know how to operate.

Parents must be familiar with whom their children are communicating. We must know their online and cellular friends just as we know the friends in their class, school, or in the neighborhood. There are billing options that allow you to see the numbers of the people that communicate with your child. You can also determine the times of those communications. The times can help you determine if your child's cell phone use is very late at night or during class. Parents need to look at and become familiar with whom and when your child is using their cell phone.

Cell phones may also be a safe way for your child to seek assistance when involved in or witnessing an act of bullying. They can reach out to family, friends, or even a school office to report incidences. Just as cell phones allow us to call for police or fire rescue in an accident or time of need, cell phones can be an easy way to report an incident to someone who can help without putting a child at risk of being called a snitch or tattletale. We must foster discussions that help children learn what to do when they aren't sure what to do but know that something is wrong or inappropriate. Remind them that you or another adult is just a phone call away when they need help. It would be helpful to program important numbers into the cell phone that a child might need such as the school or an anonymous reporting line.

Fact #54 Text messaging can be a link or a tool to exclude or hurt others. (Kowalski & Limber, 2007)

Gaining the Peaceful Edge . . . "Texting," the practice of typing messages with the cell phone to send a message to someone else, has become a very common activity.

The use of text messaging and other global communication media has made exposure to cyberbullying more commonplace and children are no longer safe when in the proximity of adults. Children and teens have become text-messaging experts and can text under a desk or table and send rather lengthy messages in a short period of time. Cell phones allow kids to receive and send messages in seconds. We must be aware how, what, when, and where our kids are communicating and that exposure to violent, mean, and bullying text messages may put a child at a risk equal to or greater than face to face exposure to similar behaviors.

Kids may also be at risk for mimicking these bullying behaviors they frequently witness. This may lead to desensitization, so that bullying becomes part of the daily routine and climate of a school. When using text messages, children must understand that the same rules apply that are outlined for e-mail, phone, and Internet use.

The same courtesy and respect that you would be expected to give to another when face to face should be expected when communicating electronically. Positive friendships and relationships need to be fostered by focusing on an ethical code that is based on mutual respect.

Many children think that text messages disappear and are only between the sender and recipient or recipients. Let them know that they become part of the virtual word and can be retrieved if necessary. Additionally, messages may be forwarded and shared with others for whom they were not intended. Also it is important to note that word processing allows for additions and deletions that may alter the meaning of a text without permission, care, or thought. So, tell kids to beware!

Fact #55 Internet blogs and chat rooms can be a place to vent emotion but at the same time they can be very public. (Chibbaro, 2007)

Gaining the Peaceful Edge . . . Introduce a journal or other more private means of keeping personal feelings and information rather than on the Internet.

When a word is said it cannot be taken back. When it is said at home it is heard by a few people; when it is said at school it is heard by a larger group, but when it is said on the Internet there is no limit to the number of people who have access to that information. The old saying that "some things are best left unsaid" is especially true when it comes to placing information on the Internet. Unless you are perfectly content having something shared with millions of people of all ages all over the world, you shouldn't post it anywhere on the Internet.

Blogs and chat rooms should be used with extreme caution. Information shared may become great ammunition for those involved in cyberbullying. Even worse, the information can be misconstrued and used to hurt others. Statements made in anger or immaturity can turn children against each other and create a hostile online environment. Even worse, manipulating birthdates can expose children to sexual, cruel, and inappropriate material. Your child may think they are chatting with someone who claims to be their age but may really be a child predator.

Children must learn not to share personal information virtually, and that means feelings and thoughts as well. Adults should investigate and monitor any blogs or chat rooms that their child wants to visit online. We wouldn't allow children to enter places that exposed them to alcohol, drugs, guns, and other risks and dangers. Likewise, we should be discriminating concerning the virtual places children and teens visit.

Fact #56 Cyberbullying can be both direct and indirect. (Roberts, 2005)

Gaining the Peaceful Edge . . . Whether the student is actively origi-nating the cyberbullying or making someone else do it, they are still responsible.

The computer provides an opportunity to change the game of bul-lying. There are some who prefer to write the nasty e-mail or send ed-ited photos to others, and there are those others who pass those mean messages along. The truth is that those others become just as guilty as the person originating the message. There are also those kids who master getting other children to do their dirty work. We must spread the message that any and all participation is wrong and inappropriate.

Direct cyberbullying includes all instant or text messaging, e-mails, blogs, and websites used to send or post mean, nasty, and disparaging messages. This sometimes involves personal pictures that the victim may not know exist, such as a person in a bathroom or locker room. Bullies use these tools the same way they'd use e-mail—to threaten or say hurtful things. Some of these tools can include insulting or de-grading opinion polls about a classmate. Even worse, kids can involve themselves in posting another person's information online where sex-ual predators or hate groups frequent.

Fact #57 Cyberbullying has increased at alarming rates. (Beale & Hall, 2007)

Gaining the Peaceful Edge . . . As our electronic availability and capability increases, so will cyberbullying unless we teach kids about their responsibility to one another.

Cyberbullying is using the Internet or other digital communication devices to send or post harmful or cruel text or images. Technology such as cell phones help us keep in touch with our children, and the Internet assists with school and learning. However, there are many dangers that can have serious and even deadly consequences. Research suggests that over 97 percent of adolescents use the Internet, 75 percent use instant messaging, and MySpace, the most visited website, has over eighty-seven million accounts. According to the Crimes against Children Research Center, one in five teenagers in the United States who regularly logs on to the Internet says they have received an unwanted sexual solicitation. Filtering devices can help prevent your child from viewing sexual solicitations, but they don't protect from cyberbullying and cruel online social activity.

Parents need to protect their children as well as take responsibility for their use of technology. Get to know the services your child uses, and enforce what they may not use. Never allow him or her to respond to messages that are suggestive, obscene, or threatening or to send or receive messages from people who tease, taunt, humiliate, or exclude others online. This includes e-mails and instant messages that are used to make fun of others and that are sent from so-called friends.

Some cell phones allow children to take pictures and type text messages anywhere and anytime, which can allow them to bully other kids twenty-four hours a day and seven days a week. Cyberbullying can lead to cyber threats, online material that threatens or raises concerns about violence against others, suicide, or other forms of self-harm. Realize that some children use websites and e-mail to send mean text, photos, and material to threaten, ridicule, and isolate others. Remind your child that they should not respond to the cyberbullying. Consider contacting the cyberbully's parents and showing them what you received. Contact the school if it involves the school district's e-mail system or threats.

Fact #58 Even though there is clear intent to hurt the target of cyberbullying, most of the time, students do not realize the true impact of what they are doing. (Beale & Hall, 2007)

Gaining the Peaceful Edge . . . Be aware of the dramatic increase in this common form of bullying and its devastating consequences.

At times, kids may unintentionally cyberbully other students in the name of fun. It is essential that this is discussed with our children and that we help them understand the impact of these behaviors. Exclusion occurs when a child instigates friction between peers by sending messages that may cause friendships to end and even turn hateful. In the cyber world, you can reach out and touch someone negatively from the safety of your home with a click of your mouse. As cyberbullying increases, our children are at risk of becoming desensitized to the feelings of others, and bystander participation will increase.

We have even seen cases where an adult has participated in bullying a teen by posing as a high school student and sending messages that led a teen to suicide. There are people who are obsessed with the Internet and the capabilities for shopping, dating, pornography, and sex. Our children may find cyberbullying an addictive pastime, and many children will suffer and be at risk for long-term effects that may go undetected.

Fact #59 Unmonitored access to the Internet can put students in danger. (Beale & Hall, 2007)

Gaining the Peaceful Edge . . . We need to teach our children not to reveal personal information on the Internet.

Predators on the Internet are a very real and serious problem. As Internet access becomes more readily available from cell phones, virtual parties and other social networking sites are available anytime and anywhere. This availability gives greater virtual opportunity to predators to solicit potential victims. We must protect our kids by matching their technological savvy and expertise and monitoring and supervising their virtual world.

As parents, we must know our children's "online friends" just as we know school and neighborhood friends. Instruct your child to never disclose any information that may reveal their identity and to never arrange to meet online friends in person. Remind them to not open or respond to e-mail or instant messages from people they do not know. Let them know that cyberbullying is unacceptable and should be reported immediately. Share a screen name with you child; make clear rules and expectations for Internet and cell phone use. Do not have technology in your home that you have no knowledge about. When they receive unwanted messages, review how your child should respond. For example, they can simply write, "Do not contact me again, or I will contact the authorities."

Fact #60 Empathy is key to eliminating cyberbullying. (Salvatore, 2006)

Gaining the Peaceful Edge . . . Kids need to understand that by reading the cyberbullying material they are participants and equally responsible for the hurt.

When kids understand the impact of their negative actions they will be less inclined to continue. Correspondence over the Internet via e-mail, text messages, postings, and instant messaging has an informality that allows for any font and an acceptance of ignoring basic grammar and spelling. There is a lingo with shortcuts to send messages in few words and letters. This quick approach to virtual communication often leads to quick responses with little thought to how a message may be interpreted or utilized.

Empathy is something that must be nurtured and developed in our children, and our teens need regular booster shots. We must talk about cyberbullying and share stories to help kids know the hurt they may be causing one of their peers. Taking part in spreading the material by forwarding it makes them an accomplice in the bullying behaviors.

As with all bullying, this is about how we treat each other—not just kid to kid but adult to child and adult to adult. We need to show kids how we can be a good friend. Talking is important, and modeling behavior speaks volumes to kids also. It is very important to model appropriate behavior so that kids will understand the importance of basic respect and general kindness.

Fact #61 Schools have a responsibility to their students even when the cyberbullying happens after school and at home. (Willard, 2007)

Gaining the Peaceful Edge . . . Bullying is a problem regardless of where it happens, because it impacts how a student feels when they are in school.

Student learning is directly impacted when they do not feel safe in school. Online harassment and bullying may impact a child's ability to concentrate in school, their involvement in extracurricular activities, their self-esteem, and even their desire to stay in school. Schools must educate students and parents regarding cyberbullying to protect the learning environment. This means helping everyone to understand the nature of cyberbullying and how the access is infinite. Cyberbullying can and does occur twenty-four hours a day, seven days a week.

There is considerable discussion about the responsibility of the school in cyberbullying. The legal community is struggling with privacy and physical-boundary issues, while bullying, harassment, and threats in cyberspace are causing havoc in school. Many states have bully-prevention laws that mention cyberbullying. While there will continue to be discussion about exactly who should be accountable, the fact of the matter is that the school is seriously impacted.

It makes sense for schools to act by first of all having a clear policy that includes cyberbullying. This should include a procedure for reporting and investigation. Students need to know the rules about bullying. In addition, schools need to teach students about the negative impact of cyberbullying. Beyond that, schools must reward prosocial behaviors and have clear consequences for cyberbullying.

Educators should remind parents to limit their child's access to the Internet by setting parental controls and establishing reasonable rules and guidelines for computer use. Monitoring compliance with these rules by placing the computer in a family room and watching what they are looking at and with whom they are communicating is key. Teachers should be sure that computers are placed where they are visible while in use. Additionally, schools must have Internet-usage policies that prohibit cyberbullying.

REFERENCES

Beale, A., & Hall, K. (2007). Cyberbullying: What school administrators (and parents) can do. *The Clearing House, 81*(1), 8.

Chibbaro, J. (2007). School counselors and the cyberbully: Interventions and implications. *Professional School Counseling, 11*(1), 65.

Kowalski, R. M., & Limber, S. P. (2007). Electronic bullying among middle school students. *Journal of Adolescent Health, 41*(6, Supplement 1), S22.

Roberts, W. (2005). *Bullying from both sides: Strategic interventions for working with bullies and victims.* Thousand Oaks, CA: Corwin Press.

Salvatore, A. J. (2006). *An antibullying strategy: Action research in a 5/6 intermediate school.* Unpublished diss., University of Hartford, Connecticut.

Strom, P., & Strom, R. (2005). Cyberbullying by adolescents: A preliminary assessment. *The Educational Forum, 70*(1), 21.

Willard, N. E. (2007). The authority and responsibility of school officials in responding to cyberbullying. *Journal of Adolescent Health, 41*(6, Supplement 1), S64.

7

RELATIONAL BULLYING

Fact #62 Relational aggression is easy to describe but difficult to recognize. (Merrell, Buchanan, & Tran, 2006)

Gaining the Peaceful Edge . . . Relational aggression is when one student deliberately and maliciously manipulates others to exert control or to destroy relationships.

Relational aggression is the one of the most sinister and subtle forms of bullying, because the scars are not obvious on the outside. You cannot see any marks when a child is deeply hurt because the others refuse to sit with them. The target of relational aggression can be devastated and isolated because of the nastiness of another student.

Relational aggression is hard to identify, because the victims are not even sure that it is taking place. Kids can be cruel to one another; this can include those they think are their friends. When a child confides in another child and then is betrayed, we often dismiss it as just a bad day, even when the behavior is repeated. This makes recognizing this type of aggression that can have a damaging impact on a child difficult for both kids and adults.

Relational aggression can include spreading rumors, making up stories, or telling lies to hurt another. Sometimes when this comes from someone the child thought was close to them it's even more hurtful. We must support kids and help them to recognize behaviors that are inappropriate, nasty, and unacceptable. Friendships need nurturing, caring, and compassion. Kids need help in understanding what they can expect from a real friend and how to distinguish them from others that are in their social circles. It is essential for parents to help their children determine whether a relationship is worth keeping or if it is in their best interest to go their separate ways.

Fact #63 Relational bullying is very common. (Espelage, Bosworth, & Simon, 2000)

Gaining the Peaceful Edge . . . Relational aggression is so common and part of the social structure that it is hard to tell the bullies from the popular students.

Kids need acceptance, and they must feel that they have friends and fit in. For this reason, sometimes kids will go to extreme measures to be accepted and popular in their social circle. This can happen at any age but occurs most frequently in middle school. Peer groups become very important to students at that age, and kids often will bully their peers in order to "fit in."

Social position is very important, and they vie for their position. This is one of the main causes of relational bullying at this age. The interesting fact is that when teachers are asked to describe the most popular students, the descriptions are alarmingly close to their descriptions of bullies.

Many children go home and tell a parent about a certain friend who tries to get other people to bother them or to have a laugh at their expense. When making fun of other people and excluding others is left relatively unaddressed by adults, there is a tendency for the child to see it as okay. This may lead to confusion over what is bullying and what is just play.

When kids go to an adult and ask for help when dealing with issues and friends, they are often turned away and told to handle it on their own. You may recall a time when a child came to you discussing an incident that occurred with another child and you really didn't spend too much time on the issue. You may look at the children involved and not consider any of the kids as possible bullies or victims.

When children ages eight to fifteen years old name bullying as one of the biggest problems in their life, we must start paying more attention to the subtle forms like relational aggression. It only takes a few minutes to determine if a situation warrants further investigations. Additionally, the scenario may serve as an educational opportunity to discuss why certain behaviors are not in the best interest of anyone.

Fact #64 Relational bullying can occur in cyberspace. (Ybarra, Espelage, & Mitchell, 2007)

Gaining the Peaceful Edge . . . Cyberspace has become the fastest growing vehicle for relational bullying.

The virtual world has opened up the doors to bullying by allowing kids to tease and taunt each other anytime and anywhere, in ways we could never have imagined a few years ago. Students have astounding access to technology, and this access is growing by leaps and bounds.

Sometimes kids can be cruel, and this intensifies when they don't have to face their victim. When sitting in front of a computer or texting from a cell phone, it is easy to send mean and nasty messages. They become free to say anything that comes to mind, regardless of how hateful it may be, because the person is not in front of them. Kids have reported that they had no idea that they were causing so much pain and grief by their actions.

Rumors and untruths are spread around the Internet, reaching many more participants than ever possible before the introduction of technology. This intensifies the number of participants in relational aggression from one or two to a schoolwide or community. Sometimes a student could be humiliated in a class and with technology a whole group of children know about it before the next class.

Fact #65 Relational bullying can be direct. (Merrel, Buchanan, & Tran, 2006; Wolke, Woods, Bloomfield, & Karstadt, 2000)

Gaining the Peaceful Edge . . . Direct relational aggression can be dealt with by going back to the source and imposing consequences for the bullying.

In some cases, the person bullying does not even try to hide either their intentions or their actions. This is direct relational bullying. Students can be purposely mean to control another child and sabotage their relationships. These individuals utilize lies and hurtful tactics to purposely injure another child and cut them off from their social circle.

This is done directly by name-calling. We all know that kids can think of the most vile, hurtful things to say directly to one another. In addition they can communicate with gestures or looks that take an instant—most often not observed by an adult. These actions can be totally devastating to the target.

The choice to hurt another in this manner is an emotional decision. There is jealousy, anger, and resentment that often drive these decisions. In adolescents, emotions are emerging and are very powerful. It is very difficult for an adolescent to control these often wildly fluctuating emotions. From this emotional point, they can make choices that are antisocial and harmful to their peers. These actions can, in turn, have a serious impact on the target. Research tell us that relational bullying causes depression, social anxiety, loneliness, physical symptoms, and in some cases suicide.

Direct relational bullying often becomes something that others look up to and want to model. If this is allowed to continue without consequences, this can lead to an increase in the amount of peer abuse in our youth. Again, it leads us to a common theme, that we must encourage empathy and work on creating a positive school culture where all children belong and the infliction of psychological harm is given the same consequences as physical.

Fact #66 Relational bullying can be indirect. (Merrel, Buchanan, & Tran, 2006)

Gaining the Peaceful Edge . . . Indirect relational aggression is when one student uses others to hurt a peer's friendships and social status.

Indirect relational bullying is a most insidious form of bullying. This is when a student chooses to manipulate others to hurt or exclude another student. "If you want to be my friend, you cannot sit with her." Or "My friends think she is a sleaze." Others, looking for approval, act on this direction and actually become the bullies doing the work of the indirect bully. This type of indirect bullying can also happen when a person seems nice in the presence of the target but changes their tune when the target is out of sight.

This type of bully is clever in orchestrating others to participate so that bystanders as well as adults have a difficult time really understanding what is happening. It is awful to think that our children have difficulty identifying these direct and damaging behaviors.

For example, one student may see another girl talking to her boyfriend. In an instant, she is outraged and jealous. It only takes a few words to someone else or a quick e-mail to all her friends and soon everyone has been told that she is a boyfriend stealer. (Of course today students would use much stronger, more vulgar descriptive adjectives.)

It is easy to identify a physical fight when someone walks up to another person and punches them in the nose, but less easy to recognize punches that are words directed at a child's character and reputation.

When a child's main source of popularity is gained by making fun of others and working feverishly to have others excluded, we have a dangerous situation. Kids realize that standing up to a person like this will make them an automatic target. This fear encourages the tormentor to continue the cycle of bullying, and the victim is often unsure why it is happening as the person seems to be nice to them when they are around them.

As adults we need to go to the source of all bullying incidents. It may not be clear who is at fault, which makes relational bullying difficult to identify and correct. We need to follow through with observations and questions to determine the source of the problem.

Fact #67 Whether you call it relational aggression or social aggression, it is just mean! (Lacey, 2007)

Gaining the Peaceful Edge . . . Whether or not it is boys or girls who resort to social aggression, the result is the same; the victim is hurt.

We really need to understand exactly what being mean is, and we should not underestimate this form of aggression. There must be intent to do harm, the behavior needs to be perceived by the victim as harmful, and there needs to be an imbalance of power. Even though we cannot see the marks, relational aggression leaves emotional bruises. This bullying happens when the target is attacked verbally (or with gestures) through intimidation, social manipulation, or exclusion.

One of the reasons relational aggression is so common is because peer group relations are extremely important to children. A student's position in the social strata is crucial, so they will do whatever it takes when they are jockeying for popularity. This happens with boys as well as girls. Interestingly enough, students describe the popular kids with the same adjectives as they use to describe bullies!

By putting down a peer, a student can feel as if their social status has been elevated. Kids try very hard to associate themselves with groups, and there is always an "in" group who holds the top rung on the social ladder. These are the students who wield power over their peers.

They have discovered numerous ways to make the lives of their peers miserable and turn their school environment into one of depression, isolation, and fear. In school settings where this behavior exists, students may even eventually be bullied out of their academic potential and left feeling unwanted and unliked.

Fact #68 Boys are least likely to report bullying, and many do not see relational aggression as a problem. (Xie, Farmer, & Cairns, 2003)

Gaining the Peaceful Edge . . . Because they fear embarrassment and retaliation, boys are the least likely to report bullying.

Generally speaking, boys do not see anything wrong with verbal teasing and bullying. Some researchers have found that younger boys are more aggressive than girls because it is more socially acceptable. When children become adolescents, the relational bullying equalizes between boys and girls.

It is not until the bullying becomes physical that many boys see it as a serious matter. This may be attributed to gender expectations that boys should be tough and get over any hurt feelings. Unfortunately, this leaves many boys to suffer when they are the victim of relational aggression and feel helpless in escaping the torment. In addition, peer rejection is often closely associated with physical bullying. It is as if some boys get a dose of two forms of bullying.

When a boy reports relational bullying, it is often dismissed unless it escalates to physical bullying. Reporting the bullying may make it worse, and the victim may seem even weaker in the eyes of their peers and the adults around them.

There is also an issue regarding tattling and reporting for many of our children, especially our boys. For many boys, being a snitch or tattletale is worse than anything else imaginable. We must help our kids to understand that reporting and tattling are two different things and that nonphysical forms of bullying exist and may cause just as much or more suffering than the physical.

Boys who use relational aggression often do not understand the impact this hurtful and mean behavior has on their peers. They do not realize that name calling, social exclusion, and the other forms of relational bullying can be devastating to their peers. It is essential to develop empathy among all students so that they will understand the impact of their behavior on the victim.

Fact #69 Relational aggression can lead to physical aggression and bullying. (Underwood, Galenand, & Paquette, 2001)

Gaining the Peaceful Edge . . . The cycle of escalation can be reduced when relational bullying is consistently addressed.

In a moment, relational aggression can escalate. Words, gestures, exclusion—any of these forms of bullying can lead to a heated exchange, or these feelings can fester until a later point in time. For a child who may be impulsive, response to hurt emotions can easily become physical. The psychological harm done by relational aggression is no less harmful than physical aggression and bullying, yet adults often do not respond until it is physical.

We know that the average act of bullying takes thirty-seven seconds and that the majority of these instances are nonphysical. This leads to a climate that is hostile and volatile. Most adults are not even aware of these occurrences. Adults only respond in one out of twenty-five incidents of bullying—and most of those incidents are physical. While there are many reasons why adults do not respond more often, it is clear that most of the responses are provoked when the bullying becomes physical. Not responding gives kids some level of tacit approval for bullying.

Relational aggression has the intent to injure, with the same imbalance of power found in physical bullying, and is often a more acceptable ways for girls to be mean to each other. This type of aggression can become physical, and then the damage may go beyond psychological harm and include bodily harm as well.

Fact #70 Best friends are the very best defense against relational bullying. (Hodges, Boivin, Vitaro, & Bukowski, 1999)

Gaining the Peaceful Edge . . . Helping children to develop friendship skills is the best defense against bullying.

To help protect a child from becoming a victim, it is imperative to help them find a friend, because there is safety in numbers. When a child has a best friend or group of friends, they are less likely to feel like they are being targeted or will be left in a vulnerable situation. Adults should help foster friendships so that no child is left alone at recess or lunch time.

Children must be taught what constitutes a friend so that they may select good friends and be a good friend. Teaching a child the difference between a true friend and an acquaintance is a good first step. A friend is someone who would come to your home and spend time together with you and who respects you and your things. A buddy is someone who is in school in the same class or on the same team. Finally, an acquaintance is someone you recognize from school. Reinforcing these categories helps children to understand how to identify their real friends.

As parents, we should not ignore the social side of school or the importance of your children's friends. If we want our children to strive academically, we must help them survive socially. Bullying can delay or stop the learning process, as well as cause long-term psychological distress. It is imperative that we give kids the best defenses against bullying, and that includes a best friend.

Fact #71 Sticks and stones will hurt you! (Nishina, Juvonen, & Witkow, 2005)

Gaining the Peaceful Edge . . . Name-calling is just a hurtful as physical bullying.

Kids need to know that the words they say and actions they take have may have long-term and damaging effects on others. To reduce bullying we must go back to the basics of what is right and wrong when it comes to treating other people. There is a fine line between joking and really hurting someone.

Teasing and joking happen between children of equal power. They are friends before the teasing and they will be friends afterward. If the behavior continues and one student asks the other student to stop, it must. Whether this becomes bullying or an argument is determined by the balance of power between the students at that time.

It is common today to hear children say "I didn't mean it" or "I didn't know it was mean; I was just kidding." Bullies are often very shrewd when they are confronted with their behavior, and it is no different with relational aggression. Since most of the time bullying behavior is not directly witnessed by an adult, it is difficult to identify the source.

Unfortunately, there is a sphere of influence in the media and video games that works against efforts for tolerance and respect for others. Just as in bullying prevention, where awareness of the seriousness of the problem is an essential component to being successful, awareness is necessary for kids to understand hurtful actions.

We must help identify a global understanding of what is mean, hurtful, and unacceptable. We know that children are raised with different values, customs, and beliefs that may impact where they draw the line when it comes to childhood teasing. However, it would prove most useful to come up with a global code of conduct focused on peer relationships and a healthy school climate.

REFERENCES

Espelage, D., Bosworth, K., & Simon, T. (2000). Examining the social context of bullying behaviors in early adolescence. *Journal of Counseling and Development*, 78(3), 326.

Hodges, E., Boivin, M., Vitaro, F., & Bukowski, W. (1999). The power of friendship: Protection against an escalating cycle of peer victimization. *Developmental Psychology*, 35(1), 94.

Lacey, B. (2007). *Social aggression: A study of Internet harassment*. Unpublished diss., Hofstra University, New York.

Merrell, K. W., Buchanan, R., & Tran, O. K. (2006). Relational aggression in children and adolescents: A review with implications for school settings. *Psychology in the Schools*, 43(3), 345.

Nishina, A., Juvonen, J., & Witkow, M. (2005). Sticks and stones may break my bones, but names will make me feel sick: The psychosocial, somatic and scholastic consequences of peer harassment. *Journal of Clinical Child Adolescent Psychology*, 34(1), 37.

Underwood, M. K., Galenand, B. R., & Paquette, J. A. (2001). Top ten challenges for understanding gender and aggression in children: Why can't we all just get along? *Social Development*, 10(2), 248.

Wolke, D., Woods, S., Bloomfield, L., & Karstadt, L. (2000). The association between direct and relational bullying and behaviour problems among primary school children. *Journal of Child Psychology and Psychiatry*, 41(8), 989.

Xie, H., Farmer, T. W., & Cairns, B. D. (2003). Different forms of aggression among inner-city African-American children: Gender, configurations, and school social networks. *Journal of School Psychology*, 41(5), 355.

Ybarra, M. L., Espelage, D. L., & Mitchell, K. J. (2007). The co-occurrence of Internet harassment and unwanted sexual solicitation victimization and perpetration: Associations with psychosocial indicators. *Journal of Adolescent Health*, 41(6, Supplement 1), S31.

8

MEDIA AND VIDEO VIOLENCE

Fact #72 There is a connection between witnessing violence and bullying. (Bonanno, 2007)

Gaining the Peaceful Edge . . . If you limit the child's exposure to violence, you are actually preventing bullying at the most basic level.

Research shows that kids watch an alarming amount of violence on a daily basis. Since 2001, the American Academy of Pediatrics has recognized the exposure to violence in the media as a significant risk to the health of children and adolescents. Adults must be or provide the role model for our children. We have standards for educators regarding ethics and the professional code of conduct supporting the importance of exposing children to positive behaviors.

Although we may not be able to block all our kids' exposure to violence, we can take an active role in monitoring the amount and intensity. We certainly wouldn't intentionally allow children exposure to drugs, alcohol, and pornography, so why would we not emphasize the exposure to other health risks? Don't be afraid to set limits and be selective regarding what your children view in the media. Children need and crave parameters, and they look to the adults in their life for direction.

As a community, we must recognize the impact of violence on youth and its contribution to school climate, bullying, and risky behaviors. We must establish a shared vision to identify initiatives that limit risk factors and commit to educating children in violence prevention and providing entertainment options that promote empathy and nonviolent expression. We must build connections that help children and adolescents understand their role in creating a safe and positive community.

Fact #73 The average kid watches two to four hours of hours of television per day—and by the time they enter kindergarten they will have witnessed eight thousand murders. (Huesmann, 2007)

Gaining the Peaceful Edge . . . Do not underestimate the impact of media violence on children.

Kuntsche (2006) found that watching more than two hours of television per day was associated with higher risks of verbally aggressive behavior, such as name-calling and spreading rumors. Parents must limit unsupervised television viewing. Promoting participation in extracurricular activities and organized sports may be a great alternative to leaving kids unsupervised with television and Internet access.

Television and watching violence on television are neither the cause of bullying nor the reason that children and adolescents exhibit violent behavior. However, exposure to violence should be minimal, as there is reason to be concerned about the impact of this exposure. Desensitization, modeling, and a lack of empathy may be associated with long-term exposure to violence on television. As parents, we have become more tolerant about what is acceptable for children. There are movies that are rated okay for children thirteen and older that just twenty years ago would have certainly been rated only suitable for adults.

Reading, playing, drawing, and daydreaming have beneficial effects for children. Creativity, reflection, and vocabulary building are some of the outcomes from leisure activities other than television and video games. We should be reminded that speaking with our children about school and their day promotes success at school. Additionally, these conversations allow you to stay informed about the challenges, worries, and concerns in your child's life. Thus, make it a priority to limit television and electronic media and to shift some of your children's time to other constructive and healthy alternative activities.

Fact #74 When violence is committed by the hero, violence is justified, sending a negative message. (Huesmann, 2007)

Gaining the Peaceful Edge . . . To counterbalance that message, remind children that real violence hurts real people.

Often the hero in children's television uses violence to defeat the bad guys and save the victims. For instance Power Rangers, Ninja Turtles, and Transformers teach that violence by good guys is acceptable. We underscore peaceful problem-solving and conflict-resolution options to counteract exposure to violence as a heroic solution to problems and disagreements. We must shift the mindset that physical or mental negative actions are viable options for success.

Youth are exposed to war, terrorism, and violence occurring around the world, and this may create fear and emotional cutoff to death, killing, and injury associated with war. What is the culture in our schools, home, and community? Do we promote respect? Do we promote tolerance? What is the lens through which we are seen? Are we committed to promoting nonviolence? Ask yourself if you are being the model for what you want to see in your children as a parent, educator, neighbor, and leader.

We must change who we promote as role models for our youth. Children need to see monetary and status rewards for people who represent kindness, citizenship, and concern for their fellow man. If we want to change the culture of heroes and behaviors that should be recognized, celebrated, and rewarded, we must decide what we want for our children. We must get support from schools and communities to begin the slow process of changing what we have unintentionally supported in our kids. We must recognize that this is a slow process, and it may take many years of campaigning and lobbying for others to recognize the importance.

Fact #75 Television violence rarely depicts any consequences and frequently rewards aggression. (Worthen, 2007)

Gaining the Peaceful Edge . . . When talking with children, it is important to highlight the courage and rewards of real heroes—for example, firefighters and policemen.

Children who are exposed to violence get the message that it is okay and a usual part of the world. We, as adults, may struggle with detachment from the realities of violence. When we hear about real-life tragedies involving death, murder, and casualties of war, we try to block the reality and finality of death and violent acts. On any given day we may turn on the news and hear about a bombing or other terrorist act with multiple civilian casualties and then turn it off and not think about it. We know that to survive mentally we must move past tragedy and block haunting thoughts that may cause anxiety and depression. Although such self-preservation may be healthy at times, it leaves us vulnerable to desensitization to the devaluing of human life.

It is possible and quite important to promote a healthy and age-appropriate concern, compassion, and empathy for those who are suffering or who have been victimized by violence. An example is exposing our children to heroes in our community, such as the paramedic who performs life-saving acts for someone in need and the fireman who saves an entire neighborhood from fire damage. Seek opportunities for children to participate in efforts to help those in need or to assist with projects in the community.

Fact #76 Violence in the media fosters a culture of meanness. (Worthen, 2007)

Gaining the Peaceful Edge . . . Stress the virtue of kindness to counterbalance the negative effect of meanness and violence.

There are many messages the media depicts, and children are vulnerable to all of them. When children continually witness jokes and comedy at the expense of others, they may associate fun with making fun of others. Mean and rude behavior in the name of comedy and good fun send the message that it is okay and is even a great way to be cool and popular. Many times when children exhibit bullying behaviors by making mean comments, they are surprised when the hurt they inflicted is mentioned. Many kids say that they were just joking and really didn't mean to hurt another person.

We must discuss and point out behaviors that are mean, rude, and unacceptable forms of entertainment. We must prevent kids from saying that they didn't know or didn't mean it. Whether they meant it or not, the hurt can be done and, if allowed to continue, may cause long-term negative effects for the victim. Praise, respect, and appreciation should be promoted, and we must define the fine line between bullying and joking around. The more we talk about this, the more we can teach our children to think before they speak and act and to put themselves in another's shoes.

Today, we are so busy teaching children so many things. We want to provide opportunities for sports and exercise, music and art to make them well-rounded, fit individuals. It is essential that we put that same time and energy into their character and develop an awareness and appreciation for themselves and others. Kindness is contagious, so we must expose them to it as often as possible.

Fact #77 Kids who play violent video games tend to be more hostile and aggressive. (Konijn, Nije Nijvank, & Bushman, 2007)

Gaining the Peaceful Edge . . . It is a fact that many video games have violent content.

When our children are growing, we often take precautions to ensure that they are growing and developing properly and receiving adequate nutrition. We recognize that little bodies need rest and proper nutrition to grow and develop. Limits are placed on junk food and soda to promote a healthy lifestyle. We must do the same thing with their intellectual growth and development and screen the video games that our children play. While some are educational, others are graphically violent.

Some people say that playing video games is an outlet for aggression. Actually the exact opposite is true. Playing video games gives children a way to practice aggression. It is a virtual role-play. They can not only try on the role of the aggressor, but they also can more closely identify with the aggressor by playing these games over and over. Children and young adults who play these games become insensitive to the violence that is occurring in the game with repetition. The victims become objects or things that feel no pain. They are not real and therefore can be crushed, mutilated, dismembered, or killed at the flick of a thumb.

It is no surprise that children become immune to violence or that there is a link between aggression and the favorite video game of kids today. Find out exactly what your child is playing and how often. Many parents feel comfortable that their child is just playing video games and not being exposed to mature subjects before their time, but not all video games are created equal, and parents must become informed consumers.

Fact #78 The effects of violence in the media are long term! (Hues-mann, 2007; Slaby, 1995)

Gaining the Peaceful Edge . . . By focusing on the long-term effects of exposure to violence, we as adults can understand the importance of limiting a child's exposure.

There have been many studies that have verified the importance of limiting the exposure to violence in television. The long-term effects are very serious. It is about what viewing violence teaches children and young people. They learn that violence is everywhere and seldom has consequences. When it comes to the "good guys" they learn that violence is justified. Heroes can even use unrestrained violence as revenge. This then becomes the profile of a good guy.

Now think of the Road Runner or the Three Stooges. Here the violence is funny, and there is no connection to the physical consequences of the violence. It is common for children to reenact the violence they see, and, when it comes to violence based in humor, someone is likely to get hurt even though the intention is to be funny.

As is demonstrated by years of research, there is a clear correlation between watching violence and violent behavior. Children who watch more television and are therefore more exposed to media violence are more likely to have committed serious crimes by the age of thirty.

In general, violence in television or movies can increase fearfulness in some children. They can develop nightmares and become afraid of loud noises or the dark. Many times, interrupted sleep patterns can be traced back to movie or television violence. Or children and young adults can become insensitive and accept violence as a normal part of life. What is even more frightening is that the more they are exposed to violence, the more violent the next movie or television show will have to be to keep their attention, and so the appetite for violence increases.

The important thing to remember is that empathy is the cornerstone to reducing bullying. If we are exposing kids to violence through various media we are sending them a mixed message about our values.

Fact #79 Monitoring television viewing and screening video games is a way to reduce a child's exposure to violence. (Bushman & Anderson, 2007)

Gaining the Peaceful Edge . . . Watching television with children and having a discussion about what they are watching is a great way to help children understand about violence.

Children in the United States watch an average of three to five hours of television every day. This leaves very little time for reading, creative play, and communication with family. Studies also indicate that by the time they graduate from high school, children have spent eighteen thousand hours watching television, compared with thirteen thousand hours in a classroom.

Some television may be educational and pleasurable for children, but parents should be aware of the potential effects of excessive viewing, such as violent behavior, poor academic performance, precocious sexuality, obesity from being sedentary, and exposure to drug and alcohol use. Television news and shows with violent themes may leave children scared and nervous.

If television watching interferes with reading, drawing, and exercising, it may be a major factor in preventing children from reaching their potential. Often, children watch television for lack of something else to do, so we should plan activities, read books, participate in physical activities, or just talk with each other. With proper guidelines and monitoring, television viewing can aid in raising healthy and successful students. Television watching is a choice, and parents can and should limit it.

Fact #80 Helping kids to realize the difference between make-believe and real life is important in understanding media violence. (Scaqlione & Scaqlione, 2006)

Gaining the Peaceful Edge . . . Since kids do not necessarily understand the difference between what is real and what is fictitious, it is important to explain it to them.

Preschool children love to watch television—the more action and color they see, the more they watch. They are attracted to commercials because they are fast, colorful and brief. They will watch animation as well as real figures. Children pay the most attention to violent scenes. With few exceptions, children do not understand the difference between fantasy and reality.

Children between the ages of six to eleven believe that television reflects real life. After viewing violent television shows, they will often become aggressive, acting out what they have seen. They are simply imitating the action they have viewed. They do not think in terms of cause and effect. For instance, in a television show if someone hits another over the head with a club they do not think that the person could be seriously hurt.

Young children also think of things in terms of absolutes—people are good or bad. They will identify with the good guy even if the good guy uses violence to triumph. In these times violence on television is not only common but is frequently emphasized. Children internalize what they see, and it can surface in their play. As the "good guy" they will brandish a gun and shoot the "bad guys."

To deal with this, parents can first of all limit the exposure to television. They can watch television with their children to share and understand the experience of the child. It is appropriate to comment on the activity on television by saying things like "that could not happen in real life" or "that would seriously hurt if a real person did that to someone." The understanding of the difference between reality and fantasy is a developmental issue. However, if a child is old enough to view this type of violence, they are old enough to hear about the distinction between fantasy and reality.

Fact #81 Developing empathy is crucial to helping kids understand that violence hurts and that courage is bravery and doing things to help others. (Mishna, Scarcello, Pepler, & Wiener, 2005)

Gaining the Peaceful Edge . . . The fundamental underpinning of bullying prevention is empathy, and you can teach kids about that through their media experiences.

It all begins with empathy—we can reduce and eliminate bullying by teaching kids to care about one another. This can be difficult in a world that glorifies violence, but it is our responsibility to teach kids the importance of kindness.

It is important to foster behaviors that reduce the risk of raising or promoting a bully, victim, or passive bystander. Kindness, acceptance, and appreciation for others must be taught and modeled in the early years. Children learn how to express emotions primarily through social interaction in their families and at school. Set an example of handling conflict and anger. When you are upset, do not resort to yelling, degrading others, and displaying inappropriate behavior. Small children look to adults for models of behavior. Talk about emotions, and encourage children to accept angry feelings and to deal with them in positive ways. Allow children to acknowledge all feelings, pleasant and unpleasant. The feelings are normal, but teach them how to react and interact respectfully.

Provide some opportunities for you and your child to do some community service. This gives them a chance to experience attention for kind and compassionate behavior. Unfortunately, the world often shares negative behaviors more than the positive. Allow your child the opportunity to witness others being kind.

REFERENCES

Bonanno, R. A. (2007). *Bullied to the brink: An investigation of students at risk for depression and suicidal ideation.* Unpublished diss., The University of British Columbia, Canada.

Bushman, B., & Anderson, C. (2007). Measuring the strength of the effect of violent media on aggression. *American Psychologist, 62*(3), 253.

Hazler, R., & Miller, D. (2001). Adult recognition of school bullying situations. *Educational Research, 43*(2), 133–46.

Huesmann, L. R. (2007). The impact of electronic media violence: Scientific theory and research. *Journal of Adolescent Health, 41*(6, Supplement 1), S6.

Konijn, E., Nije Bijvank, M., & Bushman, B. (2007). I wish I were a warrior: The role of wishful identification in the effects of violent video games on aggression in adolescent boys. *Developmental Psychology, 43*(4), 1,038.

Kuntsche, E., Pickett, W., Overpeck, M., Craig, W., Boyce, W., & de Matos, M. G. (2006). Television viewing and forms of bullying among adolescents from eight countries. *Journal of Adolescent Health, 39*(6), 908–15.

Mishna, F., Scarcello, I., Pepler, D., & Wiener, J. (2005). Teachers' understanding of bullying. *Canadian Journal of Education, 28*(4), 718.

Nickelodeon. (2001). Bullying, discrimination, and sexual pressures, "big problems" for today's tweens and younger kids; parents often wait for kids to raise tough issues [electronic version]. Retrieved January 22, 2008, from www.talkingwithkids.org/nickelodeon/pr-3-8-01.htm.

Scaqlione, J., & Scaqlione, A. R. (2006). *Bully proofing children: A practical, hands-on guide to stop bullying.* Blue Ridge Summit, PA: Rowman & Littlefield Education.

Schnohr, C., & Niclasen, B. (2006). Bullying among Greenlandic schoolchildren: Development since 1994 and relations to health and health behavior. *International Journal of Circumpolar Health, 65*(4), 305–12.

Slaby, R. G. (1995). *Early violence prevention: Tools for teachers of young children.* Washington, DC: National Association for the Education of Young Children.

Worthen, M. R. (2007). Education policy implications from the expert panel on electronic media and youth violence. *Journal of Adolescent Health, 41*(6, Supplement 1), S61.

9

CONSEQUENCES AND
LEGAL RAMIFICATIONS

Fact #82 It is important to distinguish the difference between bullying, threats, and harassment. (O'Shaughnessy, Russell, Heck, Calhoun, & Laub, 2004; Cornell, Sheras, Kaplan, McConville, & et al., 2004)

Gaining the Peaceful Edge . . . While we have to take bullying seriously, in most states bullying is not a legal term.

While we have increased awareness and programs in schools to deal with the subject, in most states bullying is not a legal term. Bullying encompasses a lot of different behaviors, and some may be illegal under federal, state, civil, or criminal laws. Sometimes, there is no line between sexual bullying and sexual harassment, as some behaviors can be both. A behavior does not necessarily stop being bullying and then become sexual harassment. We must think about whether the behavior meets the elements of one or the other, neither, or both. There are specific forms of harassment: Sexual harassment is based on gender or sexual orientation. Racism is harassment and/or discrimination based on race or ethnicity. Harassment can also be based on religious beliefs and disability.

These forms of harassment can occur in many different ways, including peer on peer, staff on student, or staff to staff. In other words, it can happen at many different levels. There is a continuum, a line that can move from bullying to harassment, but certainly harassment can occur independently of, and/or simultaneously with, bullying. Harassment is a breach of the law and must be treated as such.

While the law is quite clear on these matters, it is very difficult to find the line between bullying and harassment. Since not all states have laws that address bullying, some people do not consider it enough of a problem to warrant intervention. However, if bullying is effectively handled at the earliest levels, harassment and other violent behaviors will dramatically decrease.

Fact #83 Bullying cannot be mistaken for sexual harassment. (McGrath, 2006; Rallis, Rossman, Bocc, Regan, & Kuntz, 2007; Willard, 2007)

Gaining the Peaceful Edge . . . Sexual harassment begins with actions that are directed toward a student's gender or sexual orientation.

Title XI of the Federal Education Amendments of 1972 prohibits sexual harassment as a part of discrimination. This can include a wide range of behaviors such as name-calling, insults, intimidation, and unwanted physical contact. Basically it involves unwanted sexual behavior that interferes with a student's right to get an education. It involves an imbalance of power between the perpetrator and the victim. Both girls and boys can experience sexual harassment.

The landmark case of *Davis vs. Monroe County* held that a fifth-grade girl had been repeatedly harassed by a boy in her grade. This has become important because it shows that a school district could be held financially responsible for knowing about a student's harassment and not taking action.

It is important to realize that sexual harassment is determined by the victim. What may be entirely benign to one person may be harassment to the victim. As with bullying, sexual harassment can negatively impact a student's academic progress, extracurricular involvement, peer relationships, and self confidence. Schools have a responsibility to protect students from sexual harassment. In fact the law is quite specific, and there is case law that holds the school liable for damages.

Schools have responded by developing policies and procedures to deal with sexual harassment. But that only manages the problem after an issue arises. We need to look at the culture that surrounds children. There is so much of a focus on sexual behavior that children do not always know what is appropriate and what is not. When they witness the constant barrage in the media, it is not surprising that harassment of a sexual nature is so common. In order to deal with this issue we need to help children understand what acceptable and respectful behavior is when it comes to peer interaction.

Fact #84 Bullying that is focused on sexual orientation can be a form of harassment. (McGrath, 2006; Rallis et al., 2007; Willard, 2007)

Gaining the Peaceful Edge . . . We need to be aware of all the ways harassment based on sexual orientation can be part of our everyday lives.

When harassment is geared toward sexual orientation, it can be cruel and absolutely devastating to the target of the harassment. When a group of fourth graders were asked to list the ways in which students could bully verbally—for example, what are some of the hurtful names used—the first answer was "gay." Some other very common retorts are "queer," "homo," and "dyke." All of these hurtful insults constitute harassment based on sexual orientation. Yet they are a very common and even daily part of the vocabulary kids use today.

The Fourteenth Amendment protects the rights of gays, lesbians, and bisexuals to be free from discrimination and harassment. We are not saying that every single time someone uses words that are related to sexual orientation that it is a violation of the law, but certainly it can escalate to that point, and school districts need to be aware of their legal responsibility to protect all their students. Therefore, language and its proper usage must be fostered to create a culture of respect for all.

When we think of bullying, we must visualize it on a continuum. It makes sense to handle it at the earliest stages—long before there is serious emotional damage and a law is broken. Like most undesirable behaviors in children, proper guidance and early intervention can prevent repeated behavior that isolates others.

Fact #85 Persistent bullying that focuses on a student's race, color, religion, or national origin can be racial discrimination. (McGrath, 2006; Rallis et al., 2007; Willard, 2007)

Gaining the Peaceful Edge . . . Bullying that attacks the race, color, or religion of another is insensitive, hurtful, and destructive for the victim.

Kids can be attacked and bullied in so many ways—their looks, size, clothes, mannerisms, and even their friends. But when the attack is directed toward a student's race, color, national origin, or religion it falls into an area where discrimination may be at the core of the issue.

Since the 1950s the courts have been very specific about eliminating racial discrimination, but it is still pervasive in schools and society today. When this kind of bullying persists it becomes harassment and becomes a legal matter. In school districts across the country Asian, African American, Hispanic, and even Caucasian students still experience this in some form, even though we are very conscious as a society about racism.

Today we are mindful of the legal consequences of racism, but in many instances inappropriate comments are dismissed as simple teasing because there is a lack of intent to do harm. School efforts for multiculturalism and the celebration of diversity must be aligned with school-wide bullying prevention efforts. A fundamental value in bullying prevention is a respect and understanding of our differences.

Fact #86 Threats are not bullying. (McGrath, 2006; Rallis et al., 2007; Willard, 2007)

Gaining the Peaceful Edge . . . There is a clear difference between bullying and threats.

When a parent told the high school administrator that her son had been threatened, the administrator responded by saying "Did he say, 'I'm going to kill you,' or did he say 'I'M GOING TO KILL YOU'? There is a difference, you know." The administrator was looking to establish the intent of the speaker. However, that response to the parent was dismissive and did not address the problem. The student had been threatened and was so worried that he told a parent. In turn the parent was concerned enough to bring the issue to the school. It is apparent that the student felt threatened.

At this point, the administrator should investigate to determine the nature of the issue and then make decisions based in those interviews. Dilemmas such as this may be part of a larger problem of bullying that has escalated to threats. It is important for schools to consider, in advance of any problems, the difference between bullying and real threats. This will be beneficial when confronted with an issue that may not be clear.

Threats can be issued over the Internet as well as in person. When a child is victimized, we must consider the impact and that bullying can sometimes be threatening as well. Parents and students should be assured that their concerns are taken seriously by schools having a protocol for dealing with these issues.

Fact #87 There is no freedom of speech when it comes to bullying. (McGrath, 2006; Rallis, et al., 2007; Schnohr & Niclasen, 2006; Willard, 2007; Ybarra, Espelage, & Mitchell, 2007)

Gaining the Peaceful Edge . . . We need to make it quite clear to children that the right to free speech ends with the first insult.

School administrators tell us that this is a common excuse when a student is confronted with something that they said. Some students feel they are protected under the First Amendment and within the right to free speech can say whatever they wish. Schools have a responsibility to respect and to teach about the First Amendment. However, schools are in the unique position to be able to restrict the speech of students. This gives schools the ability to develop and enforce clear policies that address the expectations of students.

One of the areas unprotected by the First Amendment is "fighting words." These are expressions that by their very nature are intended to provoke violence from the listener or indicate a clear and present danger of impending violence. There are words that once said are so incendiary that they evoke a violent response.

Another area is defamation of character. It is way out of bounds for anyone to think that they can say anything about someone else and believe it is within their right to free speech. Schools do not violate the student's right to free speech when they penalize this behavior.

Schools—and all adults—have the right and the responsibility to regulate expression. We do not have to tolerate the insults, threats, and fighting words of bullying behavior that offend and injure not only the victim but also the entire school climate.

We must help parents realize that some children use websites and e-mail to send mean text, photos, and material to threaten, ridicule, and isolate others. Children should be reminded that they should not respond to the cyberbullying. Parents should contact the school if it involves the school district's e-mail system or threats. Additionally, they should limit their child's access to the Internet by setting parental controls and establishing reasonable rules and guidelines for computer use. Let kids know that cyberbullying is unacceptable and should be reported immediately.

Fact #88 Teachers and other school personnel can be part of the bullying problem. (Lipson, 2001; McGrath, 2006; Rallis et al., 2007; Tremlow & Fonagy, 2005; Willard, 2007)

Gaining the Peaceful Edge . . . Bullying is an equal-opportunity offence. Adults are not immune from this problem.

Although it is difficult to discuss this topic, adult bullying of children does occur. According to the research of Tremlow, not only does it occur but it is also a major contributor to the climate of bullying. When teachers bully students there is a higher rate of student dropouts and suspensions, as well as violence within the school.

Adult bullying is when the adult uses power to threaten and intimidate a student—for example, by punishing a student through manipulation, intimidation, and humiliation. None of these tactics work. In fact, they leave a student angry and resentful. These students are more likely to repeat the very behavior for which they are being disciplined.

Furthermore, when an adult bullies a student they are modeling negative behavior. It is telling the student that this is the way to behave, giving tacit approval to the bullying tactics.

There is also adult-to-adult bullying. This can occur between parent and teacher or teacher and teacher. It is very difficult for the teacher to work in this type of hostile environment.

Any form of bullying between any stakeholders contributes to a hostile environment, which impacts the general climate. Therefore, it is very important to be certain that the school policies that are established to prevent bullying are developed to include everyone—administration, staff, nonteaching staff, parents, and of course the students. Adults must remember that they serve as role models, and adult bullying must be defined and discussed just as we must define and discuss peer-to-peer bullying.

Fact #89 Schools need to be aware of their legal responsibility in bullying matters. (McGrath, 2006; Rallis et al., 2007; Sourander et al., 2007; Willard, 2007)

Gaining the Peaceful Edge . . . Schools should no longer view bullying as a rite of passage and a part of childhood; now it is a legal matter.

Regardless of whether your state has a specific bullying law, schools need to understand that they are legally vulnerable when it comes to bullying. Therefore they need to recognize that bullying is a serious contributor to youth violence and not a normal part of childhood. Victims, bystanders, bullies, and the entire community are negatively impacted by this behavior. Bullying does not resolve itself and simply go away. In fact, school-yard bullies often grow up to be violent criminals.

Schools not only have a responsibility to deal with bullying but they are also liable if they dismiss or ignore it. This is called "deliberate indifference." The courts use this term when the school has had knowledge of and ample opportunity to intervene in a bullying or harassment incident but chooses to look the other way or to completely ignore it. Once the school has the information, they have a fiduciary responsibility to protect the victim. If they know, they must respond and take reasonable action, or by inaction they are legally vulnerable.

The best advice is to demonstrate that the school has kept due diligence. The best way to do this is to follow school policies and procedures and document every meeting and conversation. We must ensure that everyone understands that we may not view bullying as a rite of passage.

Schools are not liable for spontaneous acts of violence. Liability is with dismissing or ignoring; thus, if you know, you must take reasonable action.

Fact #90 Policies and rules are important to help define actions and expectations for preventing bullying. (McGrath, 2006; Rallis et al., 2007; Willard, 2007)

Gaining the Peaceful Edge . . . When the expectations are clear, bullying can be reduced.

We cannot just talk about bullying in the abstract. We have to make our expectations clear. At home, parents can talk about bullying. Listen to the child when they have stories from their own experiences and talk about ways in which they can problem solve. This can include involving an adult if they do not feel that the situation is safe. These conversations send a powerful message to the child about your values and expectations.

At school there must be policies that address bullying. Ideally the policy should be developed with representatives from administration, nonteaching staff, parents, and students. The policy should be broad based because there are many variations of bullying, particularly in the area of cyberbullying. It is important for the policy to allow for the changing forms of bullying. In addition, the policy needs to comply with any federal and state laws that may apply.

Basically any sound bullying prevention policy needs to include a definition of bullying. It must include a schoolwide bullying-prevention program with specific rules to support the policy. To coincide with the policy there need to be procedures for the policy that the staff can apply to the operation of the school. Once there is a policy with procedures, the school needs to have bullying-prevention training for all the staff. This will ensure that the policy will be taken seriously and show that the school is serious about bullying prevention.

The key is a focus on prevention. Once a policy and procedures have been developed, they can be enforced. This will not only reduce bullying and improve the entire school climate but it will also decrease the likelihood of legal action against the school district.

Fact #91 Bullying can be a step along a potentially lifelong continuum of escalating violence. (Boyle, 2005; McGrath, 2006; National School Safety Center, 2006; Rallis et al., 2007; Snyder et al., 2003; Willard, 2007)

Gaining the Peaceful Edge . . . It is important to think beyond the school-yard bullying to what the future can be if bullying is not stopped.

Over the past few years we have really changed our attitudes toward bullying in this country. We are much more aware of the consequences of bullying among children and young people. There are countless books on how to reduce bullying. School districts across the country are training their staff in bullying prevention. This is all very important because research has shown that unchecked bullying results in higher rates of convictions by the age of twenty-three. Bullying is a step on an escalating continuum of dangerously negative behavior.

The research is clear that bullying can lead to delinquency. We have learned that bullies are more likely to engage in delinquent activities such as vandalism, truancy, and substance abuse. Students who bully are more likely to be convicted of a crime by the age of twenty-three than those who do not bully.

Bullying in elementary school that is sexual in nature is not a stage in development, because, unchecked, it can become sexual harassment. It is no longer cute or a developmental passage—it is a serious offense that can have legal ramifications.

When kids are worried about becoming victimized, it causes stress, illness, and school phobia. When the climate is so hostile, kids need to find a way to feel safe. They will look to gangs for connection and safety from other peers. An environment that is threatening fosters the development of gangs.

Bullying that continues without any consequences can lead to date violence. Bullying is about perpetrators and victims, imbalance of power, and intent to do harm. Those are all of the components of date violence. Students who are responsible for date violence are more likely to engage in marital abuse and violence. When there is violence in the family, child abuse is likely to be present. In addition there has been a correlation between bullying and elder abuse. Again this is an extension of a behavior that was learned at an early age and allowed to continue.

Bullying can and has been carried into the workplace. Many people have stories about superiors who have abused their power and bullied them in ways that have left them frightened and uncomfortable. Bullying can begin in the school yard but can become a serious, pernicious component of our society—and the violence will continue in a vicious cycle from generation to generation.

REFERENCES

Boyle, D. J. (2005). Youth bullying: Incidence, impact and interventions. *Journal of the New Jersey Psychological Association*, 55(3), 22.

Cornell, D., Sheras, P., Kaplan, S., McConville, D., & et al. (2004). Guidelines for student threat sssessment: Field-test findings. *School Psychology Review*, 33(4), 527.

Lipson, J. (2001). Hostile hallways: Bullying, teasing, and sexual harassment in school. *American Journal of Health Education*, 32, 307.

McGrath, M. J. (2006). *School bullying: Tools for avoiding harm and liability*. Thousand Oaks, CA: Corwin Press.

National School Safety Center. (2006). NSSC review of school safety research [electronic version]. From www.schoolsafety.us/pubfiles/school_crime_and_violence_statistics.pdf.

O'Shaughnessy, M., Russell, S., Heck, K., Calhoun, C., & Laub, C. (2004). Consequences of harassment based on actual or perceived sexual orientation and gender nonconformity and steps for making schools safer. Retrieved January 25, 2008, from www.casafeschools.org/SafePlacetoLearnLow.pdf.

Rallis, S., Rossman, G., Cobb, C., Reagan, T., & Kuntz, A. (2007). *Leading dynamic schools: How to create and implement ethical policies*. Thousand Oaks, CA: Corwin Press.

Schnohr, C., & Niclasen, B. (2006). Bullying among Greenlandic schoolchildren: Development since 1994 and relations to health and health behavior. *International Journal of Circumpolar Health*, 65(4), 305.

Snyder, J., Brooker, M., Patrick, M. R., Snyder, A., Schrepferman, L., & Stoolmiller, M. (2003). Observed peer victimization during early elementary school: Continuity, growth, and relation to risk for child antisocial and depressive behavior. *Child Development*, 74(6), 1881.

Sourander, A., Jensen, P., Ronning, J. A., Niemela, S., Helenius, H., Sillanmaki, L., et al. (2007). What is the early adulthood outcome of boys who bully or are bullied in childhood? The Finnish "from a boy to a man" study. *Pediatrics*, 120(2), 397.

Tremlow, S., & Fonagy, P. (2005). The prevalence of teachers who bully students in schools with differing levels of behavior problems. *American Journal of Psychiatry*, 162, 2,387.

Willard, N. E. (2007). The authority and responsibility of school officials in responding to cyberbullying. *Journal of Adolescent Health*, 41(6, Supplement 1), S64.

Ybarra, M. L., Espelage, D. L., & Mitchell, K. J. (2007). The co-occurrence of Internet harassment and unwanted sexual solicitation victimization and perpetration: Associations with psychosocial indicators. *Journal of Adolescent Health*, 41(6, Supplement 1), S31.

10

BEST PRACTICES

Fact #92 Bullying prevention should involve increasing positive behaviors by rewarding kindness! (Fonagy et al., 2005)

*Gaining the Peaceful Edge . . . A peaceful school environment is one
that encourages, values, and rewards positive behavior.*

Studies have shown that programs that focus on reducing violence
and encouraging positive behaviors can effectively decrease bullying
behaviors. Students learn better when they are in an environment in
which they feel comfortable and safe. The focus needs to be on the
entire school environment.

While it is very important to deal with individual incidents of bullying
when and where they happen, intervention is not prevention. The general climate is fundamental to prevention. When the climate is hostile or
indifferent, bullying is more likely to continue and thrive. Schoolwide
programs address the school climate by presenting a unified approach to
bullying prevention. This includes not only consistent consequences for
bullying behavior but also recognition of positive behavior.

One of the important components of a schoolwide plan is to reward
prosocial behaviors. We cannot always be telling kids what we do not

want them to do, we have to give them direction about our expectations for good behavior. Some schools have regular programs to recognize kids "caught doing the right thing." This can be anything from a formal effort to something as simple as a verbal compliment. We need to tell them when they have done the right thing. For instance "I saw that you sat with Emily at lunch today—that was kind of you because she does not seem to have many friends." That simple acknowledgement sends a powerful message about values.

We can also influence kids by pointing out honorable actions by characters in literature. Reading about real heroes in both fiction and history and then discussing them with the child again sends the message that the certain attributes of the hero are ones that can be applied to their own life. For instance—the life of Martin Luther King, Jr., is one that was founded on respect for others. You can talk with kids about how they can apply that concept to their own lives. It is in these conversations that you can help kids understand the underlying foundation of character that helps them to make the right choices.

Fact #93 Schools need to understand what works and what doesn't in regard to bullying prevention. (Vreeman & Carroll, 2007)

Gaining the Peaceful Edge . . . The best bullying-prevention programs work to improve the entire school climate.

Effective bullying prevention begins as proactive programs that work toward establishing a safe, friendly, and caring social environment. It takes much more effort to reduce bullying than simply punishing a student's mean and hurtful behavior. While it is very important to take bullying seriously and to address it immediately, this is really intervention rather than prevention.

Therefore, bullying-prevention programs must be multifaceted. Vreeman and Carroll (2007) conducted a literature review of studies of school-based bullying interventions. They looked at the direct outcomes of bullying, such as bullying, victimization, aggressive behavior, and school responses to violence, as well as the indirect outcomes of bullying.

This review showed that school-based interventions that worked on changing school climate did have a direct impact on the frequency and severity of bullying behavior. This is good news, because if the goal is to have students feel safe in school, working to improve the climate is essential.

The most important question a school needs to ask when assessing a bullying-prevention program is whether or not it is research based. This is the best indicator to determine if the program will be successful. While there are many programs, there are only a few that can demonstrate success based in long-term research with many schools in various settings.

Schools need to know that empathy development is very important in reducing bullying. However, it is never a good idea to put the bullies in a group to discuss their behavior. This just strengthens their resolve and reinforces the behavior. It can even give them the opportunity to exchange ideas about bullying. Strategies that include groups for bullies are not very successful.

Peer-mediation and peer-counseling programs may work well, but they were not designed to handle bullying situations. Peers have equal power. Bullying is about an imbalance of power. It is when the victim cannot, for many different reasons, defend himself. Therefore it takes an adult to intervene and to solve these issues.

Fact #94 Zero-tolerance policies are not effective in reducing bullying in schools. (Skiba et al., 2006)

Gaining the Peaceful Edge . . . Even at home zero tolerance as a form of discipline does not work.

In the literal definition, zero-tolerance policies are when there are severe and harsh punishments for certain specified behaviors. These policies are nonarbitrary in nature—in that they have no provisions for extenuating circumstances. Policies that mandate punishments and are severely punitive foster resentment and take away the student's opportunity to learn. Policies that mandate and severely punish disruptive students regardless of the nature and degree of the offense can actually increase negative behavior.

Research has shown that schools are not any safer when they have zero-tolerance policies. The discipline rates are the same—but more importantly, students do not learn from the discipline. The consequence for the negative behavior may not be in proportion to the offense, leaving the student angry and resentful—and likely to continue the behavior. Degrading treatment and unfair punishment are not good discipline.

Zero-tolerance policies do not consider students' true mistakes with momentary bad decisions or their impulsivity. Nor do they consider peer influence that may force a student's participation. In these instances there may not be intent to do harm.

In any setting, discipline should teach in order to reduce repeat behavior. We need to focus on giving kids the tools they need to succeed in their peer environment. Prevention strategies should include all students to improve school climate. In addition, we must be aware of students who may be at risk and specifically target those students.

There need to be clear rules about what is unacceptable behavior. These rules should to be available to all, including students and staff. It is important to know that consequences for bullying and other negative actions are very important in reducing the behavior. However, they need to be consistent yet allow for flexibility according to the circumstances and seriousness of the offense.

Fact #95 Avoiding harsh discipline assists with bullying prevention!
(Christie, 2005)

*Gaining the Peaceful Edge . . . Discipline should never be harsh; the
purpose of discipline is to teach.*

The goal of discipline should always be to teach. It should never be
meted out in anger, with the intent to humiliate or to harm. We know
that violence should never be a response to violence. Adults should try
to avoid physical or harsh discipline. Children exposed to hostile behavior usually have poor problem-solving skills.

One of the major risk factors for a child to exhibit bullying behaviors is an autocratic form of discipline used in the household. These
children may have emotionally absent parents who don't take the time
to really communicate. Discipline must include listening and offering
constructive guidance rather than reactive consequences.

Consistency is essential when it comes to discipline and teaching
children how to handle conflict. Being consistent and age-appropriate
is necessary. Parent involvement and supervision does not only reap
academic benefits. Bullying behaviors decrease when a child has parents who nurture, listen and understand in combination with appropriate limits and boundaries.

Fact #96 Empathy counteracts bullying! (Ward, 2007)

Gaining the Peaceful Edge . . . Kindness toward others is a very important tool in bullying prevention.

For both boys and girls, low empathy has been related to bullying—violent bullying by boys and indirect bullying by girls. The community and schools should be actively looking for ways to foster empathy, cooperation, and self-control.

We must help children and adolescents recognize the feelings of others and try to relate them to their own personal experiences. When we start to think about the way our actions and words may affect those around us, we are better prepared to express ourselves in a kind and respectful manner. Promoting empathy and kindness is not an overnight process. This must be embedded in the curriculum at school and reinforced to parents and the community so that it becomes part of the culture and over time a norm for kids.

It is important to teach your child empathy for others. Share how you feel when you see others exhibit bullying behaviors. Talk to kids about how verbal assaults, cyber attacks, gestures, and mean facial or eye expressions can be cruel. They can hurt as much or even more than physical hitting.

Fact #97 Schools can play an active role in protecting kids from the long-term affects of being victimized by bullies. (Sourander et al., 2007)

Gaining the peaceful edge . . . The school is as important as the parent in detecting bullying in order to protect children from the long-term negative effects of bullying.

Schools are in the best position to observe children and understand how well they are adapting, as well as how they are developing socially. Teachers and school staff see children on a daily basis. They know more about these children, including whom they socialize or may be having difficulties with, than sometimes the students' own families. Children who are stressed from bullying will frequently go to the school nurse for assistance or shelter from the difficulty they may be facing in the classroom.

Teachers and staff often know which children tend to be more isolated, and, most importantly, they know which children do not have good friends. This is crucial in identifying children who may be at risk. The teacher can then help the child make friendships and relationships with some of their peers. Having a friend or friends helps support children who may be victimized. In instances where the problem needs special attention or services, the school can help refer the child to the appropriate person, agency, or source.

In addition, the school can focus on the culture and the importance of developing a healthy sense of respect for others. Lessons can be addressed throughout the curriculum; for example, in literature classes, teachers can focus on the relationships between the characters in the story and how that relates to the definition of a real friend. They can talk about how one can develop friendship skills and how to help a friend who may be a victim of bullying.

Schools can serve as resources for parents to help them foster healthy friendships and reinforce themes of respect, empathy, and kindness modeled in the school. Parent involvement is an important component of promoting academic achievement. This is also true for emotional growth and instilling basic values.

Fact #98 Help kids to develop good friendship skills. (Kevorkian, 2006)

Gaining the Peaceful Edge . . . Kids need to know how to be a good friend so they will know how to recognize one.

For most kids, making friends is easy—but there are some that have a bit of difficulty. We cannot assume that it is easy for all children to know how to make and keep good friends. Therefore we need to discuss with a child just exactly what a good friend is.

Conversation with the child is important; ask questions that encourage them to think about the special qualities they like in a friend. Does the friend have the same interests? Are they in the same class or sports team? Is the person happy and has nice things to say? How do you know a person is kind and friendly?

You can point out how friends treat each other in the movies and television and in literature. These are the times when the child will listen, because the information is not about them—rather, it is about the character. When the discussion is not about them directly, kids are more likely to talk about their feelings.

Role-playing where kids can try out their friendship skills is not confined to school. For instance, the parent can help a child try out different ways to integrate into a play situation. For us as adults this looks like a very easy thing—but for a child, it can be difficult to know how to ask.

Parents can also be a good role model for the child by treating others respectfully. It is important to make it clear that while everyone will not be a friend, we have to treat everyone with respect. That includes being polite and courteous!

Also, you can practice problem solving. For instance, what would you do if you wanted to play with some kids that were already playing a game? How can you ask for a toy that someone else is using? What would you do if someone is not nice to you? By asking these questions and having a discussion you can give the child the opportunity to think out ways to handle these situations before they are actually in a similar situation.

It helps them to really understand how to be a friend. This is very important, as children need to understand who they can consider a real friend. Bullying prevention is about bystanders learning to protect their friends. So understanding how to be a friend is a very important first step in having good friends.

Fact #99 Know your school before you begin a bullying-prevention program. (U.S. Department of Health and Human Services, n.d.; Whitted & Dupper, 2005)

Gaining the Peaceful Edge . . . Before beginning a bullying-prevention program, it is best to survey students and staff to better understand the extent of the problem.

There are four basic components of a schoolwide bullying-prevention program. First of all there needs to be an assessment of the bullying problem. In order to deal with the problem you must know the four Ws—where, when, who, and what.

Schools need to know where bullying is happening. Most of the time, bullying occurs in areas that are not directly supervised. These areas can include the cafeteria, playground, bathrooms, or the school bus. However, a survey may reveal areas within the school in which bullying frequently takes place. In fact, some surveys have revealed that bullying can happen in the classroom—right in front of the teacher!

Schools need to know when bullying is happening. When asked, students will tell you when bullying is most likely to happen. This may be during specific times in the day, such as the change of class when kids are in hallways with minimal supervision. Bullying can also occur during a specific class where there is less structure, such as art or gym.

It is also important to know who is doing the bullying. Is it happening between students in the same class? Is it happening between boys and girls? Is it happening between students of the same sex? This will also tell you if adults are responsible for the bullying—which is crucial information when developing a bullying-prevention program.

Finally, it is most important to know what type of bullying is happening. We now recognize that bullying can take many different forms. It can be physical, relational, direct, and indirect. Bullying can happen via electronic means or by a simple look or a gesture.

The best way to get this information is to survey the students. There are several good instruments on the market to get this information. These surveys have been designed to look at this information as well as to examine attitudes toward bullying. When you understand the students' attitudes toward bullying, you can get an idea of the level of empathy for the victim. When there is low empathy, there is high probability that the bullying will continue. Whether you use a formal survey or devise one on your own, you can use the information to make crucial decisions about your bullying prevention program.

Fact #100 Good schoolwide bullying-prevention programs have ten basic components. (U.S. Department of Health and Human Services, n.d.)

Gaining the Peaceful Edge . . . Bullying prevention takes time and determination, but you can make a difference.

There are many excellent bullying programs that are research based. But they all have some fundamental elements. According to the Health Resources and Services Administration's Stop Bullying Now Campaign, there are some basic components to "Best Practices in Bullying Prevention and Intervention."

1. *Focus on the social environment.* This important because it takes a very respectful and caring atmosphere that does not allow bullying.
2. *Assess bullying at your school.* It is key to determine when and where bullying occurs to be able to plan to address this issue.
3. *Garner staff and parent support.* It takes a village to raise a child—and it takes the same village to reduce this type of abuse.
4. *Form a group to coordinate the school's bullying-prevention activities.* In order to guarantee the continuation of a bullying-prevention program, it is important to have a group of people who will monitor progress.
5. *Train your staff in bullying prevention.* It is very important to have a common understanding of bullying in order for all to respond consistently.
6. *Establish and enforce school rules and policies related to bullying.* There need to be universal rules that are clear and readily available to everyone.
7. *Increase adult supervision in hot spots where bullying occurs.* Adult presence is an excellent deterrent to bullying. It is important to know the areas where bullying is happening and adjust supervision accordingly.
8. *Intervene consistently and appropriately in bullying situations.* Interventions need to be regular, with all adults responding respectfully according to the bullying prevention rules.

9. *Focus some class time on bullying prevention.* This is the opportunity for students to have discussions about their concerns about bullying as well as to learn how to handle the bullying.
10. *Continue these efforts over time.* Bullying prevention is not a one-time event. It is a process that must be planned to be ongoing.

Fact #101 Bullying prevention is a community endeavor.

Gaining the Peaceful Edge . . . Bullying prevention needs to involve all of us.

Bullying is a behavior that has existed as long as there were school yards for children to gather and play. Today, the playing field has changed; the tolerance level for certain behaviors varies and often serves as a catalyst for bullying behaviors. The lack of adult intervention in regard to bullying has created a sense of acceptance for these behaviors. When adults and caregivers do not respond quickly and appropriately to the behavior, they tacitly approve of it.

How the community responds sends messages to our children about violence and appropriate behavior. There are some instances in which adults encourage the behavior by telling the child to hit back or retaliate. But violence is never a good response to violence; in fact, it can and will escalate the behavior. By telling the child to fight back, we are contributing to a climate of violence.

It is the climate that influences behavior for good or bad. In other words, a climate of respect does not foster bullying. When all those involved, both the children and adults, understand and treat each other with respect, there is no place for bullying. Respect becomes the norm, and bullying behavior is unacceptable. When children who are looking for peer and adult approval recognize that this will come by treating one another civilly, the bullying will cease.

But it takes all of us—everyone who has contact with the child. It begins at home with families who are kind to each other. Caregivers and educators need to demonstrate kindness and empathy when dealing with children. Any form of bullying must be addressed immediately with clear and appropriate sanctions. Most importantly, all of us need to employ respect and consideration when dealing with our peers.

We can eliminate bullying. It takes all of us working together to teach and model the behavior we want to see now and in the generations to come. We can encourage kids to make good choices, choose kind friends, and become proactive and responsible in defending their peers by joining as a community to the set the tone.

REFERENCES

Burns, S. (2006). School bullying in Northern Ireland: It hasn't gone away you know [electronic version]. Young Life and Times Survey. From www.ark.ac.uk /ylt/2005/.

Christie, K. (2005). Chasing the bullies away. *Phi Delta Kappan, 86*(10), 725.

Delfabbro, P., Winefield, T., Trainor, S., Dollard, M., et al. (2006). Peer and teacher bullying/victimization of South Australian secondary school students: Prevalence and psychosocial profiles. *British Journal of Educational Psychology, 76*, 71.

Fonagy, P., Tremlow, S., Vernbert, E., Sacco, F., & Little, T. (2005). Creating a peaceful school learning environment: The impact of an antibullying program on educational attainment in elementary schools. *Medical Science Monitor, 11*(7), CR317.

Kevorkian, M. (2006). *Preventing bullying: Helping kids form positive relationships.* Lanham, MD: Rowman & Littlefield Education.

Skiba, R., Reynolds, C., Graham, S., Sheras, P., Close Conoley, J., & Garcia Vazquez, E. (2006). Are zero-tolerance policies effective in the schools? An evidentiary review and recommendations. Washington, DC: American Psychological Association. From www.apa.org/ed/cpse/zttfreport.pdf.

Sourander, A., Jensen, P., Ronning, J. A., Niemela, S., Helenius, H., Sillanmaki, L., et al. (2007). What is the early adulthood outcome of boys who bully or are bullied in childhood? The Finnish "from a boy to a man" study. *Pediatrics, 120*(2), 397.

U.S. Department of Health and Human Services. (n.d.). Best practices in bullying prevention and intervention. From stopbullyingnow.hrsa.gov/HHS_PSA /pdfs/SBN_Tip_23.pdf.

Vreeman, R. C., & Carroll, A. E. (2007). A systematic review of school-based interventions to prevent bullying. *Archives of Pediatric and Adolescent Medicine, 161*(1), 78.

Ward, S. K. (2007). *Patterns of discrete social skills among incarcerated middle school youth with bullying and victimization problems.* Unpublished diss., University of Illinois at Urbana-Champaign, United States.

Whitted, K., & Dupper, D. (2005). Best practices for preventing or reducing bullying in schools. *Children & Schools, 27*(3), 167.

ABOUT THE AUTHORS

Meline Kevorkian, Ed.D., is the author of *Preventing Bullying: Helping Kids Form Positive Relationships* and *Six Secrets for Parents to Help Their Kids Achieve in School* and she is coauthor of *The Comfort Zone: Providing a safe and bully free environment for School-Age Child Care*. Currently, she is executive director of Academic Review at Nova Southeastern University, a Board Member of the International Bullying Prevention Association, and a columnist at *The Miami Herald* (Broward).

Meline presents regularly on best practices in bullying prevention, cyberbullying, as well as numerous topics facing educators, parents, and students in today's schools. Her experience includes teaching and administrative positions in both public and private schools from preschool through the University level. Her research focuses on best practices in bullying prevention, school safety, and academic achievement. She has been featured on the Today Show, CNN, NBC, WSVN, Mom Talk Radio, WLRN Public Television, BlueSuitMom .com, and the National PTA.

Robin D'Antona, Ed.D., is a Certified National Olweus Bullying Prevention Trainer, president and executive director of the International Bullying Prevention Association, and coauthor of *The Comfort*

Zone: Providing a safe and bully free environment for School-Age Child Care. Robin is an educational consultant for the Cape Associates and works with school districts, after school programs, and other groups training parents, teachers, coaches, and practitioners about bullying prevention.

She is the former associate director of the Project on Teasing and Bullying at the Center for Research on Women of the Wellesley Centers for Women. She was a program consultant to the Commonwealth of Massachusetts Bullying Prevention Project expansion schools. She has dedicated her career to training and research to raise awareness and further the information base of the negative effects of bullying.